BLOOMFIELD TOWNSHIP PUBLIC LIBRARY

3 1160 00383 5662

EA 8/18   EA 1/04

The Pearl Book

The Definitive Buying Guide

How to Select, Buy, Care for & Enjoy Pearls

by
Antoinette L. Matlins, PG

D1301523

GemStone Press
Woodstock, Vermont

BLOOMFIELD TOWNSHIP PUBLIC LIBRARY
1099 Lone Pine Road
Bloomfield Hills, Michigan 48302-2410

The Pearl Book: The Definitive Buying Guide
How to Select, Buy, Care for & Enjoy Pearls
© 1996 by Antoinette L. Matlins

All rights reserved. No part of this book may be reproduced or
transmitted in any form or by any means, electronic or mechanical,
including photocopying, recording, or by any information storage
and retrieval system, without permission in writing from the publisher.

Library of Congress Cataloging-in-Publication Data
Matlins, Antoinette Leonard.
The pearl book: the definitive buying guide: how to select, buy, care
for & enjoy pearls / Antoinette L. Matlins.
p.   cm.
Includes bibliographical references and index.
ISBN 0-943763-15-0 (pbk.)
1. Pearls. 2. Pearls — Purchasing. I. Title.
TS755.P3M38   1995
639'.412 — dc20   95-36880

Grateful acknowledgment is made to the individuals and organizations
who supplied photographs for use in this book. Please see "Credits" in
backmatter for credit information.

Front cover design & interior design concept: Glenn Suokko
Color photograph section design: The Laughing Bear Associates

10 9 8 7 6 5 4 3 2 1

Manufactured in the United States of America

GemStone Press
A Division of LongHill Partners, Inc.
P.O. Box 237 / Sunset Farm Offices, Rte. 4
Woodstock, VT 05091
          Tel: (802) 457-4000
          Fax: (802) 457-4004

To my daughter Dawn
And granddaughter Bryn

Like the finest of pearls

May your spirits radiate from within,

And shine forth with a soft glow.

May they reflect an inner quality and beauty

That transcends the surface...

And stands the test of time.

JUN 0 4 1997 B & TAYLOR

BLOOMFIELD TOWNSHIP PUBLIC LIBRARY
1099 Lone Pine Road
Bloomfield Hills, Michigan 48302-2410

Table of Contents

Acknowledgments   vii

Introduction   viii

Part One   **Pearls: First Among Gems**   I

Chapter 1   Most Ancient of Gems, Most Precious of Gems   3
Chapter 2   Legendary Pearls, Legendary Tales   14

Part Two   **What Is a Pearl?**   21

Chapter 3   Pearls in the Making   23
Chapter 4   Different Types of Pearls: 38
     A Pearl for Every Mood

Part Three   **The Difference Quality Makes**   57

Chapter 5   Quality — Key to Lasting Beauty   59
Chapter 6   Artificial Enhancements Used   76
     on Lackluster Pearls

Part Four   **Selecting Pearls to Treasure**   85

Chapter 7   How to Choose Fine Pearls   87
Chapter 8   Pearl Choices — A World of Variety   90
Chapter 9   Pearl Prices — Some Guidelines   100

Part Five   **Lustrous Advice from Illustrious Experts**   III

Chapter 10   The Experts Speak   113
Chapter 11   Great Jewelers on Great Pearls   134
Chapter 12   Magnificent Auctions Highlight   148
     Magnificent Pearls

Part Six   **Wearing and Caring for Pearls**   157

Chapter 13   Wearing Pearls with Style   159
Chapter 14   Caring for Pearls to Keep Them Lustrous   166

Part Seven   **Important Advice Before and After You Buy**   169

Chapter 15   What to Ask When Buying Pearls   171
Chapter 16   Good Insurance Requires a Good Appraisal   176
Chapter 17   Getting a Laboratory Report   179

Where to Go for Additional Information   187

Selected Readings   188

Practical Pearl Glossary   190

Credits   193

Index   195

Price Guides

American Cultured Freshwater Pearls	101
Cultured Saltwater Pearl Necklaces	102
Baroque Cultured Saltwater Pearl Necklaces	105
South Sea Cultured Pearls	106
Freshwater Rice Pearl Necklaces	106
Mabé Pearls	107
Tahitian Black Cultured Pearls	108

Special Charts

Nacre Thickness	67
Grading Nacre Thickness in Japanese Pearl Strands	69
Misnomers and What They Really Are	83
Popular Uniform Necklace Lengths	165
Popular Graduated Necklace Lengths	165

Color Photograph Section   following page 118

Acknowledgments

A Special Thank You

To my father, Antonio C. Bonanno, FGA, MGA, PG, I would like to say a very special thank you. Thank you for providing a model of honesty and integrity, for caring so much, and doing so much, to enlighten those who share your passion about gems. And thank you for the hours we spent together when I was a child, with George Frederick Kunz's magnificent *Book of the Pearl* in your lap, reading to me, and showing me "real" examples from your own collection. I know that if you had been able, this book is the one you would have especially enjoyed writing with me, and so it is specially dedicated to you. With love.

I would like to express my deep appreciation to Gina Latendresse, John Latendresse and Salvador Assael for emphasizing the need for this book, for encouraging me to write it, and for their technical review; to Devin Macnow, for including me in so many pearl seminars over the past few years, from which I was able to get a clearer picture of the kind of pearl information that was really needed; to *Pearl World,* and to the Cultured Pearl Information Center, for their assistance in obtaining current information on worldwide pearl production and visual materials; to the South Sea Pearl Consortium, for their assistance in obtaining the latest information about South Sea pearls, and for providing photos; to Joan Rolls, for her help in obtaining visuals and information on Cook Island pearls; to Antiquorum Fine Auctioneers, Christie's and Sotheby's for providing photos of historical or exceptional pearls; to TelePress Associates for providing bridal and fashion photos; to Richard Drucker for his help in compiling price information; to the many experts, jewelers and designers who gave so generously of their time in permitting me to interview them, or sending me comments and experiences to share in this book.

I would also like to express my gratitude to

Karen Bonanno DeHaas, FGA, PG
Kathryn L. Bonanno, FGA, PG
Kenneth E. Bonanno, FGA, PG

— fine gemologists, but who, being sisters and brother as well, couldn't let me write a book without putting in a word or two of their own!

And my heartfelt thanks to Barbara Briggs for all the late nights at GemStone Press, and to my editor, Sandra Korinchak, for her "pearls" of wisdom and "brilliant" suggestions, all of which have added a more lustrous quality to *The Pearl Book!*

Introduction

Pearls have always held a special allure for me. Perhaps it's their almost spiritual quality; perhaps it's their quiet, regal elegance; perhaps it's the many different moods each pearl possesses, reflecting my own. Perhaps it's knowing their beauty is truly of nature's own making, a beauty that stands on its own, unenhanced by humankind.

Whatever the reason, I love pearls. And, interestingly, it is a love shared by my husband, who cares little for diamonds or most other gems. The most important gifts he has bestowed upon me have all been pearls. My most cherished possession is an exquisite natural pearl and diamond ring he gave me to wear next to my wedding ring; I wear it always. I don't know what it is about them that draws him, but his appreciation for pearls, and the pleasure he experiences seeing me in them, mirror my own appreciation and pleasure in wearing them.

This is an especially exciting time for anyone who loves pearls. There are more types of pearls available today than ever before, in every color, shape and price range. There are cultured pearls that cost less than $100 — and over $1,000,000! The age of the "cultured pearl" has blossomed with more varieties than have ever been seen before, and *new* varieties just appearing; pearls now rival the finest diamonds, rubies, emeralds and sapphires, set in jewelry that is nothing less than fabulous.

It is the *best* of times...and it is also the *worst* of times. I say this for one very important reason: poor quality pearls are being sold that look pretty today, but which will LOSE THEIR BEAUTY IN A VERY SHORT TIME. Unfortunately, many pearls being produced will *not* stand the test of time; some will lose their luster in just months. Today, if you can't buy fine cultured pearls or natural pearls, I recommend that you don't buy pearls at all. Why should anyone spend hundreds or thousands of dollars on pearls that won't last? No one would, knowingly; but few understand that this can happen, or how to tell the good from the bad.

This is why I decided to write this book—to help you understand how to spot poor pearls and, more importantly, how to select beautiful pearls that will have *lasting* beauty.

There are many books on pearls, and I'm sure I have them all in my own library. None cover what I think is important, however, in terms of selecting, buying, wearing and caring for pearls. This book explains what I believe makes pearls special, what makes them beautiful, and what the important considerations should be in choosing, pricing, and caring for them; what you need to know to ensure that your pearls will become a treasured heirloom, passing from generation to generation.

I am also very pleased that, in addition to my own pearl knowledge, some of the world's most distinguished pearl authorities have accepted my invitation to share *their* expertise with you here, offering personal recollections and insights. I appreciate their time and, most of all, their confidence in me and willingness to help me make this book the best yet.

Some of the highlights include:

- A journey into the rich history and romance surrounding pearls
- Comparisons of natural, cultured, and imitation pearls:
  what they are, how they differ, and how to separate them
- How to look at pearls to properly judge quality
- A look at pearls from all around the world, with practical
  and aesthetic comparisons
- What to guard against: artificial enhancement and
  misrepresentation
- Pearl prices — from affordable to stellar
- Magnificent pearl jewelry from the world's leading jewelers
- How to wear and care for pearls
- Insider "tips" from world-renowned industry experts
- And more...

It is my hope that this book will open your eyes to pearls as never before. I hope it will show you how to feel more confident about the pearls you select, how to care for them, and how to derive enjoyment from them for years to come. Perhaps it will even spark a little flame that will become a passion such as mine; one that will last a lifetime.

— Antoinette L. Matlins, PG

Part One
Pearls: First Among Gems

Top left: Queen Elizabeth I,
the Pearl Queen

Top right: Queen Henrietta Maria
(1609-1699), wife of King Charles I
of England. Note the "Mancini" pearl
earrings (see Ch. 12), and the pearl
necklace.

Left: The "Prince of Pearls":
The Rana of Dholpur.

Chapter 1

Most Ancient of Gems,
Most Precious of Gems

**"The richest merchandise of all, and the most soveraigne
commoditie throughout the whole world, are these pearles."**
– C. Plinius Secundus (Pliny the Elder), Roman historian
and writer, from *Natural History,* 77 A.D.

The allure of the pearl is timeless and universal. Since the
beginning of recorded history, the pearl has been extolled as a metaphor for life itself, for virtue and love, wisdom and justice, spirituality
and righteousness. Always regarded as one of the rarest, most valuable
and symbolic of all gems, its praises are sung by the great poets of every
age; it is praised in every culture, from ancient China, India, Persia, Egypt,
Greece and Rome, to the Mayan, Aztec and Incan cultures of the Americas, and even the ancient cultures of the South Pacific and Australia.

The illustrious history of the pearl is unparalleled. Today's
birthstone for June, the pearl has a history more ancient, more fascinating, more spiritual, and more regal than any other gem. The portrait
collections of the world's great museums most vividly illustrate the unri-
valled reverence and prestige reserved for the pearl. Here, as one strolls
through the generations, we can see that in every age, history's most
illustrious men and women chose to be adorned in *pearls* for the images
they wished to leave to posterity. What could more dramatically highlight the allure of the pearl than seeing that from among all of their
riches, the pearl was the gem of choice.

The world's greatest literature has extolled the value and virtue of the pearl. We find it in the most ancient of Chinese books; in the

ancient sacred books of the Hindus; the Bible; the Talmud; the Koran; Dante; Shakespeare; in the writings of the greatest Roman historian, Pliny, from whom we have learned so much about the gems of the world and the beliefs surrounding them up to that time.

In the modern world fine pearls continue to evoke a sense of awe and wonder, perhaps even more so because of our understanding of how the pearl is actually created. For many, the pearl is seen as a very beautiful and poetic metaphor for life. In a world where we often wonder how we will survive the obstacles and stresses that threaten to overwhelm us, the pearl is an exquisite reminder that from something which might at first appear to be misfortune can come something of great beauty and value, something that would not otherwise have been created at all. For, as you will see, the pearl itself is something that would never have been created without adversity and struggle! And perhaps even more important, whether or not there will be a pearl at all, and the *quality* and *beauty* of the pearl, depend upon what the individual mollusc *does* to deal with the situation; not all molluscs in the same situation create a pearl, and of those that do, not all create something beautiful. And so it is in life.

We don't know exactly when or where the pearl was discovered, but it is likely that it was long before recorded history, probably by someone searching for food, possibly a member of an ancient fish-eating people. Whatever the case, there is little doubt that the pearl was highly valued from the very first, for a beauty as unique as its origin.

Unlike diamonds and most colored gemstones, its beauty is there for all to behold from the very first moment. It needs no enhancement; it needs no cutting or polishing. A fine pearl has a depth and lustrousness that seems to actually glow from within. Imagine how it must have seemed to an ancient people when one of their clan, perhaps while eating or shucking a mussel, discovered a shimmering, round, glowing pearl! In an age when people worshipped the forces and elements of nature as gods, when amulets and talismans were more precious than all other things, imagine not only the surprise, but the awe and mystery that must have surrounded the moment. Imagine what must have gone through their minds when they beheld this *natural* beauty, coming as a gift from a *living creature*, radiating a lustrousness that must have seemed nothing less than a *living spirit*!

It is not difficult to believe that the pearl was truly the first *gem* — something beautiful, rare, and highly prized. To ancient peoples who believed that inanimate objects possessed special powers that could be transmitted to the owner or wearer, a pearl — coming from a living sea creature and exhibiting an inner glow suggestive of life itself — must surely have seemed a treasure more powerful and more valuable than all else!

Earliest Known Cultures Prize the Pearl

"If in life you gave no alms, In death how do you deserve a pearl?"
– China, *Chuang Tzu*, c. 2350-625 B.C.

We will probably never know exactly when or where the moment of discovery occurred, but we know the pearl has been revered since the beginning of recorded history. In Asia we find evidence dating back thousands of years. In the over-4,000-year-old book *Sho King (Chuang Tzu)*, there are numerous references pointing to the importance of pearls. Here we find mention of a pearl from the Yangtze River being presented to the Emperor Yu in 2206 B.C. We are told of kings bearing gifts of pearls, of pearls in tax records, and of pearls after death. In a Confucian ode written here the important question is asked: *"If in life you gave no alms, In death how do you deserve a pearl?"* Here, so long ago, we find the pearl associated with charity, and the hope of a such a reward incentive enough to lead a good life. This may be the first recorded testament to the connection between pearls and virtuous acts.

In China we also have accounts dating back about 1,000 years telling of the popularity of small mother-of-pearl–coated Buddhas, which were cleverly created by inserting thin lead castings into freshwater molluscs to obtain a pearly coating. We don't know why, but there may well have been a spiritual significance.

The rulers of ancient India and "Ceylon" (now known as Sri Lanka) also valued the pearl, and we discover in ancient writings dating back 2,500 years that pearl fisheries were known off the coasts of Ceylon at that time, and that pearls were highly valued. Here we find pearls considered an important enough gift to send with emissaries from Ceylon to India to assure friendship between the rulers of these lands.

While little pearl fishing now occurs in Ceylon, we know it flourished throughout the Roman period because the Roman historian Pliny makes specific mention of Ceylon as the major source of pearls "par excellence." The Persian Gulf became a source for pearls from about 300 B.C., and quickly became the source of the most highly desired pearls, the most beautiful of all, discovered off the islands of Bahrain. The Persian Gulf remained the major source of most of the world's important pearls from that ancient time until the mid-20th century. There are portraits of Persian kings and queens adorned in pearls, and the Louvre houses a necklace containing pearls and other gems that dates from at least the fourth century B.C.

The conquests of ancient Persia over Egypt and Greece probably resulted in the introduction of pearls to these parts of the world — pearls are strongly associated with Aphrodite, the ancient Greek goddess of love — and, through Greece and Egypt, to Rome and other parts of the world. During the Roman empire we find pearls also strongly associated to Venus, the Roman goddess of love; the close link between *pearls* and *love* is clearly an ancient one. These early conquests may also have contributed to the increase of pearl fisheries in the Red Sea along the coasts of Arabia and North Africa, important sources of pearls at that time, although extinct today.

Margaret — A Real Pearl

The Romans loved pearls and the women displayed them lavishly; the Roman passion knew no bounds. None, however, made a greater show than did Pompey, who in his triumphal procession displayed his own likeness created of pearls. For the Romans, pearls were one of the most sought after of all the riches from the East. Wealthy Roman women would sleep on beds inlaid with pearls to assure a peaceful night's sleep. Toward the end of the Roman period, when "sumptuary laws" were put into effect to try to limit vulgar displays of wealth, an individual could not wear more than the prescribed number of pearls at one time. According to Pliny, in the first century A.D. pearls ranked *first in value* among all precious things.

The Romans used two words for "pearl." If large and perfect, the word *unio* was used, meaning unique. Romans also used the word *margaritae* (from the Greek word for pearl), indicating something cherished or of unusual value. The name "Margaret" in all forms — Marguerite, Margarita, and so on — means "pearl." Since Roman times it has come to be associated with the pearl-like qualities of purity, spirituality, virtue, and chastity.

Pearl, Perle, Paarl, Perla...

The word "pearl" is similar in many languages — in English (pearl), French and German (*perle*), Dutch and Swedish (*paarl*), Italian and Spanish (*perla*). This word, universally recognized today, probably came from the Roman word *pirula* meaning "tear-shaped," as were many of the natural pearls known to the Romans. The word *pirula* spread throughout Europe with the spread of the Roman Empire, and, as it was used to describe the shape of many natural freshwater pearls, probably came to replace the word *unio* to describe this natural beauty.

Pearls for the Bride — An Ancient Tradition

"And Krishna brought forth pearls from the depths of the sea to give to his daughter on her wedding day."
– The Rigveda, Ancient Hindu Book, c. 1000 B.C.

As we mentioned earlier, some of the most ancient records relating to the pearl are found in Ceylon and India. Long before the Romans were enjoying pearls, the pearl was held in high esteem in India. Pearls are mentioned often in ancient Hindu writings, in the sacred texts known as the Vedas. These provide some of the earliest mentions of pearls associated with longevity, prosperity and preservation of life. Here the word *krisana* appears — almost 3,000 years ago — translated as "pearl". Here we also find the story of *Krishna*, the *preserver* (notice the similarity to the word "*krisana*"). And here, also, we find perhaps the oldest written mention of pearls in association with weddings. We are told how Krishna *brought forth pearls from the depths of the sea to give to his daughter on her wedding day*. What a beautiful story. What a rare and magnificent gift. And what better illustration of the pearl's great value. The Hindu story is perhaps the earliest mention of pearls and marriage...and the start of a centuries-old tradition of pearls as the appropriate adornment of the bride!

Left: Here, the Russian Czarina at the turn of the century.
Right: The pearl is the "wedding gem" today, as it has been for hundreds of years.

The ancient Greeks also believed that pearls should be part of the wedding experience; believing that pearls would help ensure marital bliss and prevent newlywed brides from crying, they were considered "the wedding gem." During the period of the Crusades, we find that pearls were the gift of many a gallant knight returning from the Middle East, bestowed upon his "fair lady" for her wedding day. By the fourteenth and fifteenth centuries, we find pearls at the height of "wedding fashion" with royal weddings in the House of Burgundy taking place in a veritable "sea of pearls." Historical accounts document that virtually everyone from the bride herself to her male guests were adorned in glistening pearls.

From Queen Elizabeth I to our modern Queen Elizabeth II, the tradition has continued through the centuries (see Chapters 2 and 12). At the beginning of the 20th century, pearls were as much a nuptial gem in the United States as diamonds are today; pearls accounted for over 75% of jewelry sales in the U.S. at the turn of the century. Today, the tradition of bestowing pearls upon the bride for her wedding day, often by the father of the bride, or by the groom himself, continues as it has for hundreds of years.

Pearls and the Kingdom of Heaven

In addition to the bride, other references from the Hindu Vedas evoke exquisite images with pearls. The Rigveda extols, *"Savitar comes! The God from the far distance, And chases from us all distress and sorrow, His chariot decked with pearl."* And again, *"Like a dark steed adorned with pearl, so the Fathers have decorated heaven with constellations."*

In the earliest Jewish writings the pearl appears often as a metaphor for those things which were most highly valued. In the ancient Biblical text of Job, for example, we find that in describing the value of *wisdom*, it is emphasized by placing it above all other things of value, including the *pearl*.

We also find in the Jewish literature the wonderful rabbinic story of Abraham and his wife Sarah entering the land of Egypt. Here Abraham, when confronted by customs collectors, is willing to part with all of his valuable possessions — even pearls — to protect Sarah, whose love he places at an even higher value. The value of pearls, we see in this story, is second only to love, the most valuable of all things.

By the beginning of the first century, we begin to see references to pearls in Christian writings. Starting in the New Testament, with the book of Matthew, the kingdom of heaven is likened by Jesus to a single pearl of great value — *"The kingdom of heaven is like unto a merchant man, seeking goodly pearls; Who, when he had found one pearl of great price, went and sold all he had, and bought it."* Later in Matthew we are told, *"Give not that which is holy unto the dogs, neither cast ye your pearls before swine."* The twelve gates of heaven — the "pearly gates" — we read about in Revelations: *"And the twelve gates were twelve pearls; every several gate was one pearl; and the street of the city was pure gold, as it were transparent glass."*

Pearls are also closely associated with the Virgin Mary and Jesus. Early Christian writings refer to Jesus as "the great Pearl" brought forth by Mary. As the most valuable of all things known at the time, a more highly revered, more highly valued image could not have been found.

By the sixth century, the allure of the pearl is undiminished. According to Islamic mystics, the pearl was the first creation of God, and for Moslems the pearl is a special gift to the world from God. For this reason, Moslems hold *natural* pearls in very high regard and often avoid cultured pearls altogether.

A Persian manuscript illustration showing Shah Sulaiman (1647-1694) bedecked in pearls and seated on a pearl-studded carpet.

We find the great prophet Mohammed (570-632) commenting on the pearl's beauty and value in the wonderful imagery he used in the Koran, the sacred book of Islam. For Mohammed's followers, it would not have been possible to imagine greater rewards than those he describes to followers of Islam when describing Paradise: *"The stones are pearls and jacinths; the fruits of the trees are pearls and emeralds; and each person admitted to the delights of the celestial kingdom is provided with a tent of pearls, jacinths, and emeralds; is crowned with pearls of incomparable luster, and is attended by beautiful maidens resembling hidden pearls."* Today, Moslems around the world continue to value pearls highly, and fine pearls rank among their most cherished possessions.

Pearls for Health

**"...most excellent for restoring the strength
and almost for resuscitating the dead."**

– Anselmus de Boot, Physician to Rudolf II (d. 1612)

In addition to its value as a gem of incomparable beauty and allure, for many centuries leading physicians believed pearls contained special curative abilities, especially for the eyes, diseases of the blood, and melancholy or depression. Pearls were believed to possess the power to enable one to see into the future, and to interpret dreams. By the 13th century they were believed to be effective for heart palpitations and diseases caused by depression. Simply by *swallowing* a concoction containing pearl, one could cure a variety of conditions. Powders were also made of pearls, and applied to the eyes because, according to an educated Castilian of that day, *"they clear the sight wonderfully, strengthen the nerves and dry up the moisture which enters the eyes."*

One particular recipe from this period sounds tasty indeed, and was reported "most excellent for restoring the strength and almost for resuscitating the dead" by its creator, Anselmus de Boot, a leading physician of the day:

> *Place pearls in a strong vinegar, lemon juice, spirits of vitriol, or sulphur, until they become liquified. Note, care should be taken to cover the glass carefully lest the essence should escape. Add more lemon juice, decant the milky liquid that results, and add sugar to sweeten. To each four ounces of this pearl liquid, add an ounce of rose water, an ounce of tincture of strawberries, and two ounces of cinnamon water. Shake well and proceed to drink from one to 2½ ounces.*

In the 14th and 15th centuries, draughts of pearl powder mixed in distilled water were given to cure insanity and other ailments. In 1492, when Lorenzo de Medici, a famous ruler of Florence, Italy, was dying of the fever, he was given a similar concoction. Reportedly, when asked by a friend to describe how it tasted, he replied, "As pleasant as anything can to a dying man." Apparently it did nothing to cure his fever; he died.

Perhaps we should not scoff, however. Not many years ago, Kokichi Mikimoto — the man who brought us the "cultured pearl" of the 20th century — when asked about his excellent health at the age of 94, commented, "I owe my fine health and long life to the two pearls I have swallowed every morning of my life since I was twenty."

In Bahrain, where by law all pearls brought into the country must be natural, some cultured pearls have been permitted by customs to enter the country — but strictly for use in *medicinal preparations* to treat cystitis, impotency, and eye problems! And in China, for example, pulverized pearls are used in cosmetic creams reported to keep skin young-looking.

The New World — The "Land of Pearls"

Most pearls continued to come from the Persian Gulf or the rivers of Europe until the discovery of the New World. Never did the crown heads of Europe dream of the wealth that would soon be forthcoming from this "primitive" land. Who could have imagined a bounty of pearls? Who could have imagined that native Americans, primitive people, were wearing fortunes in pearls! Yet we find in an ancient Hopewell Indian burial mound in Ohio, a freshwater pearl necklace almost 3,000 years old, giving testimony to the value placed on pearls by ancient native Americans.

From Europe to Asia, the heads of state were about to enjoy the richest bounty discovered in over a thousand years; a horn of plenty consisting of every type of pearl then known. The Americas were rich in exquisite freshwater pearls in every color, primarily from the lakes and rivers of the Mississippi, Ohio, and Tennessee regions of North America. In South America, the coasts of Panama and Venezuela were found to yield magnificent white saltwater pearls, rivaling the best from the Persian Gulf, and magnificent natural *black* pearls from the Baja peninsula of Mexico provided a rich bounty for kings and queens.

Christopher Columbus discovered the existence of fine pearl fisheries in the Caribbean, off the coast of Venezuela (near the island of Cubagua) in 1498. He had sent some sailors to intercept a fishing boat, curious to learn what they were catching. The men came back with pearls — described in historical writings as "large and white" — for which they had traded broken pieces of Malaga pottery. He quickly sent them back with a variety of other "modern" items, including buttons, needles, and more pottery, which they traded for about 18 ounces of pearls, a king's ransom! This area supplied Europe with an abundance of fine, large pearls until overfishing totally depleted the oyster beds.

It was not long before the courts of Europe and Asia were enjoying the luxury of pearls in full measure. By the mid-16th century, the most popular royal jewel was the pearl. Paintings of the kings and queens of Europe show them regaled with pearls, even smothering their attire, as in the portraits of King Henry the Eighth and his daughter, Queen Elizabeth the First — who even bought thousands of *imitation* pearls to meet her need to sew pearls onto every garment.

Pearls from the New World and the Persian gulf provided most of the world production of natural pearls until the early 20th century.

The Cultured Pearl Makes Its Debut

Relatively little changed with regard to the pearl market from the discovery of the New World until the 20th century and the development of the cultured pearl. While the Chinese and others had experimented with pearl cultivation for hundreds of years, it was not until the end of the 19th century that serious progress was made. An Australian named William Saville-Kent and three Japanese "inventors" — a biologist named Tokichi Nishikawa, a carpenter named Tatsuhei Mise, and the son of a noodle maker, Kokichi Mikimoto — discovered techniques for culturing pearls. In 1916, Mikimoto patented a technique to produce *round* pearls, and by 1920 he was selling them around the world.

While the name "Mikimoto" is the first that comes to mind when cultured pearls are mentioned, the Australian Saville-Kent is now believed to deserve the credit for the original development of the technique that was later found to be essential to producing a fine cultured pearl; his technique involved taking a piece of mantle tissue from one oyster and implanting it in another. His technique was perfected and patented by Mise and Nishikawa, and later purchased by Mikimoto.

Mikimoto's cultured pearl arrived at an especially critical moment in terms of the availability of natural pearls. The world supply of fine, natural pearls had already begun to dwindle significantly as a result of depletion of the oyster population from overfishing. By the mid-20th century, industrialization, the discovery of oil in the Persian Gulf, and pollution contributed to a further decline. Employment in the oil fields was also more attractive than diving because it was more dependable, and much less dangerous — there were many deaths each year connected with diving for pearls — so many divers abandoned diving to pursue work in the oil fields. It wasn't long before little remained of the world's natural oyster beds, or divers who would bring them to the surface.

Today, diving for natural pearls is done only sporadically, often by amateur collectors and treasure seekers, and the number of fine natural pearls recovered is inconsequential. The majority of fine natural pearls are now acquired from important private estates, through a private agent, or at important auctions.

Natural pearls are as rare today as at any other time in history. Perhaps even rarer. Fine natural pearls command staggering prices, placing them beyond the reach of most people. They are sought almost exclusively by collectors and connoisseurs, and people from cultures that place special value on the natural pearl, including many Arab nations.

Mikimoto and his *cultured* pearl changed the pearl market forever. Over the years, culturing techniques have been improved, and new techniques have been developed. In French Polynesia natural color black cultured pearls are now being produced, and techniques developed by Australian producers have resulted in magnificent, large white South Sea cultured pearls, which are considered by most today to be the "Queen of Gems."

Today's pearl market is a *cultured* pearl market and were it not for cultured pearls, most of us would never have seen a beautiful pearl except in the portraits of the rich and famous housed in the great museum collections. Today, for those seeking beautiful pearls, it is fine *cultured* pearls they seek.

Kokichi Mikimoto

Chapter 2

Legendary Pearls, Legendary Tales

For centuries, stories of legendary pearls have captured the imagination of people the world over, adding to their allure and stirring inextinguishable flames within the hearts and souls of adventurers and poets. These legendary treasures each carry a story almost as fabulous as the pearls themselves — tales of love, tales of hope, tales of power, tales of political intrigue, tales of search and discovery.

Antony and Cleopatra — A Costly Love Potion

The story of Antony and Cleopatra is known to be one of the greatest love stories of all time. Surpassed, perhaps, only by the story of her rare pearls.

According to legend, Antony was so taken by Cleopatra that he did everything within his power to bring her pleasure, sparing no expense. Especially elaborate were the sumptuous feasts he provided her, but at which Cleopatra simply scoffed. One day she boasted that she could easily put on a much more extravagant affair, and spend ten million sesterci (an amount equal to a king's ransom) on just one meal for him. He wagered that she could not. Cleopatra provided Antony with a lovely meal, at which she appeared adorned with a pair of magnificent pearl earrings described by Pliny to be "two most precious pearls, the singular and only [such] jewels in the world, and even Nature's wonder." Antony didn't find the meal particularly exceptional and mockingly asked to see the bill. Cleopatra exclaimed that she'd spent well over the 10,000,000, but to avoid any doubt, she removed a pearl from her ear, dissolved it in a cup of vinegar, and, toasting Antony, drank it down! A king's ransom in one swallow. She proceeded to remove the other, but the judge of the bet could not bear it, and, grabbing it from her hand, declared Antony the loser. The remaining pearl, Pliny tells us, was cut in half and made into earrings for the statue of Venus — the goddess of love of course — in the Pantheon temple in Rome, commemorating the bet.

La Peregrina — "The Unconquerable"

We aren't sure about the origins of this magnificent pearl, or exactly when it was discovered, but we notice it first in paintings of Mary Tudor on her wedding day (in 1554). Mary Tudor received La Peregrina as a gift from her husband, Philip II, King of Spain, to whom it was a gift "from America," presented to him by Don Diego de Temes. We know it came from the waters of South America, but we aren't sure of the exact circumstances. One story suggests it was found by a slave, off the coast of Panama, and because of it he was granted his freedom. Whatever the case, it became part of the Spanish treasury from the mid-1500s, where it remained until 1813. It can be seen in famous 17th century Velázquez paintings of the wives of Philip IV (Isabella of Bourbon and Mariana of Austria), and in the 1700s it gained attention at the French court of Louis XIV in Versailles, adorning the *Spanish* king's hat at the wedding of his daughter Maria Theresa to Louis. It left Spain in 1813 and went to France with Joseph Bonaparte after his abdication. A descendant, Prince Louis Napoleon, sold it to the Marquis of Abercorn in order to get out of serious financial trouble, so it found its way to England.

The marquis gave it to his wife, who had a difficult time holding onto it (it was, after all, an *undrilled* pearl, so it couldn't be fastened into a setting). It seems that on one occasion, at a ball at Buckingham Palace, she discovered it was missing from her necklace, only to spot it in the velvety folds of the train of another lady going into dinner. On another occasion, at Windsor Castle, she lost it again, but luckily found it in the upholstery

La Peregrina

of a sofa. When her son acquired it, he had it drilled.

The pearl was cleaned, polished, and weighed in 1913, at which time it was reported at 203.84 grains (there are four grains to a carat).

The pearl received tremendous publicity in 1969 when it was sold at auction by Sotheby's to actress Elizabeth Taylor for $37,000. It seems only fitting that it should have found a home with Ms. Taylor. After all, it was she who played Cleopatra, and from all descriptions, this pearl, like Cleopatra's gem, has no rival today, and is truly worth a king's ransom! Cartier Jewelers was commissioned to create a magnificent necklace to highlight this gem.

La Pelegrina — "The Incomparable"

La Pelegrina is another magnificent pearl from the Spanish Treasury. Weighing 111.5 grains, it is a perfect "egg" shape, of very high quality, with such a silvery luster that it seems almost transparent. To find a pearl of such quality, in a size so large, is truly a rarity. We know little about the origins of this pearl, but believe it also came from South America. It was a wedding gift from King Philip IV to his daughter Maria Theresa upon her marriage to Louis XIV in 1660, and thus went to France. It virtually disappears from that time until the mid-1800s, when it turns up in the Russian Imperial Treasury. It was sold in Moscow to Princess Youssoupoff and was handed down through the family. (The Youssoupoff family was an important and very influential part of the Russian royal family — it was at the Youssoupoff palace in St. Petersburg that Rasputin was murdered prior to the revolution.) In 1987, La Pelegrina was sold at auction by Christie's in Geneva for $463,800.

The "Hope" Pearl Shows That All Things Are Possible

The Hope pearl was owned by Henry Hope, the famous nineteenth century banker (perhaps best known for the "Hope diamond," the magnificent blue diamond now owned by the Smithsonian Institution). It is the largest historical pearl known, and, by virtue of its very size, certainly gives one "hope" that all things are possible. A freshwater "river" pearl, it is truly a giant. This massive pearl weighs 1,800 grains — about 450 carats, or 3 ounces — and measures 2 inches long by 4½ inches in diameter at the widest point and 3¾ inches at the narrowest

The Hope Pearl

point! It is shaped very much like the foxglove just before it blossoms, and is pure white at the narrow end, becoming a greenish-bronze color at the large end.

Hope's collection was on exhibition at the Geological Museum in South Kensington, England, for several years and was then sold in 1886. We don't know what happened to many of these pearls. In 1908, the "Hope" was offered by Garrard & Co., Jewelers to the British Crown, for 9,000 British pounds. In 1974 it was offered again privately, for $200,000.

Elizabeth I — The Queen of Pearls

"A pale Roman nose, a head of hair loaded with crowns and powdered with diamonds, a vast ruff, a vaster fardingale, and a bushel of pearls, are the features by which everyone knows at once the pictures of Queen Elizabeth."
– Sir Horace Walpole (1717-1797), novelist

When one pictures Queen Elizabeth I of England, the immediate image that comes to mind is one of a great monarch completely bedecked in pearls. It is interesting to note that she was not at all interested in wearing jewelry for personal adornment when she was young, and even later in life she cared little for any gem except the pearl. She developed a passionate love for pearls, one that knew no bounds. She covered her gowns and robes as well as herself in pearls; her love was so great that she even purchased thousands of *imitation pearls* to incorporate into her garments since the supply of natural pearls was insufficient to meet her needs. Even on her deathbed she was not without her pearls.

No one has ever loved pearls to the extent of Queen Elizabeth. She had over 3,000 gowns decorated with pearls, 80 pearl-bedecked wigs, and chests of pearl strands, rings, earrings and pendants. Dozens of grooms and pages were required to air her gowns daily and dust and polish the jewelry.

Elizabeth and the Hanoverian Pearls

Elizabeth sought the finest pearls available and obtained them from the Crown Jewels of Scotland, Burgundy, Portugal, and Navarre. She beat Catherine de Medici to the famous "Hanoverian Pearls," which by rights should have been Catherine's. Catherine had received them as a gift on her wedding day from her uncle, Pope Clement VII. She gave them to her son, the Dauphin of France, who gave them to his wife, Mary, Queen of Scots. Her collection of jewels was sold to replenish the bankrupt treasury, and Elizabeth succeeded in obtaining the exquisite pearls for 12,000 crowns. Catherine de Medici, in an effort to retrieve the pearls, wrote to request the help of the Spanish ambassador to London. He wrote back that she was too late; that Elizabeth had already gotten her hands on them!

Dating from the 14th century, these pearls (known today as the Hanoverian Pearls) consisted of six extremely long ropes of very well matched, very large, exceptionally fine pearls, and 25 loose pearls the size of small walnuts. They are considered the finest pearls in Europe. They were passed by Elizabeth to James I, and from him to his daughter, Elizabeth, Queen of Bohemia, and ultimately passed through the House of Hanover into the Crown Jewels of England.

La Régente

We know very little about this interesting egg-shaped pearl prior to the French Revolution except that it was part of the French Crown Jewels. It is a very large pearl, weighing about 337 grains (over 84 carats) with a truly exquisite shape. It was sold at auction in Geneva in 1988 for over $850,000. (See Chapter 12 for more history.)

Tiffany's "Queen" Pearl

As already mentioned, North America was a land rich with freshwater — or "river" — pearls at the time of the discovery of "the new world." Many lakes, rivers, and streams yielded lovely pearls, especially the waters of the Mississippi Valley, and although this supply was rapidly depleted to meet the demand of European royalty, the occasional natural pearl is still found today.

The largest American freshwater pearl, however, came from a place not associated with pearls: northern New Jersey. It was discovered in 1857 by a shoemaker named David Howell while fishing for mussels in a small local stream near his home in Paterson, New Jersey. While eating, he found a huge pearl weighing almost 400 grains (100 carats) on his plate — a pearl that, not knowing it was there, he had spoiled by *frying!*

Word of the find spread quickly, and a few days later a carpenter who lived nearby discovered an exquisite *pink pearl.* It weighed 93 grains (over 13 carats) and had a lovely shape. Charles Tiffany purchased the pearl and, unable to find an American buyer for this precious pearl, sold it to the Empress Eugénie, after whom it was named "the Queen Pearl." Unfortunately, in the next few years people fished the stream dry, totally eliminating the mussel population for which it had become famous, along with the lovely pearls they created.

Pearls of India — Mogul Legends

We know of the historic splendor of India (including what we call Pakistan today), and of some of its most magnificent historical pearls primarily from the writings and drawings in *Travels in India,* a book by the great 17th century traveller and writer, J.B. Tavernier. There can be no question that the rulers of India loved pearls and placed a very high value on them. Tavernier describes how pearls were used lavishly in jewelry, clothing, and even furniture. But the most vivid images are conjured up by his description of the Peacock Throne.

The great Peacock Throne, Tavernier tells us, contained many fine pearls — and the canopy under which it sat was embroidered with diamonds and pearls. Over the canopy sat the gold and gem-studded peacock from which the throne got its name. Around the peacock's neck hung a magnificent pearl, which came to rest at the center of its breast. The pearl, described as weighing 200 grains (50 carats), was suspended from a magnificent, fiery red "balas ruby" (which we know today is not ruby, but another beautiful gem called spinel).

Tavernier visited India and saw many of the jewels of the great Mogul emperors during his visits there. In addition to the pearl in the Peacock Throne, he describes five other pearls in particular — and even provides his reader with a sketch of each — one of which, he claims, had been the largest and most perfect ever discovered, with no defects whatever. He tells how it was bought in 1633 by the King of Persia, the Shaista Khan, from an Arab trader. It was shaped exactly like a pear, even having slightly concave sides, and, based on the sketch by Tavernier, weighed perhaps as much as 500 grains (over 125 carats). It is now believed that this pearl is the same as the "Sara," sold by Christie's in 1992 (see Chapter 12).

In addition to the pearl in the Peacock Throne, and the

perfect pearl mentioned above, he describes another interesting "olive shaped" pearl. This pearl, he tells us, weighed about 125 grains (over 32 carats) and was suspended from the middle of a strand of rubies and emeralds that when worn around the neck of the Mogul Emperor, hung all the way down to his waist.

Tavernier also describes what was believed to be the largest pearl ever taken from the West to the East — a pear-shaped pearl found off the coast of Venezuela near the Island of Margarita. And last, but not least, he describes a perfectly round pearl weighing about 110 grains (over 27 carats) which, he explains, the Great Mogul had never worn for lack of a match. Were he to have found a match, they would no doubt have been worn in earrings.

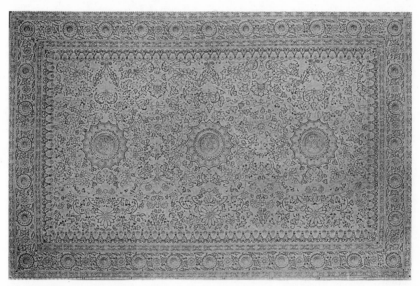

The Pearl Carpet of Baroda, a carpet of natural pearls measuring 10 feet by 6 feet, housed in the Palace of Gaekwar, and considered one of the most sumptuous, beautiful, and valuable works of art on earth.

India is indeed a land where the pearl was revered. We read of it in the ancient sacred Hindu texts; we read of it in Islamic texts; we read of it in Tavernier; and we can see today in the treasuries of India and Pakistan the finest of pearls, of every description...loose pearls and mounted, magnificent art objects, and pearl strands by the thousands.

Part Two
What Is a Pearl?

A variety of molluscs.

Chapter 3

Pearls in the Making

A pearl is an organic "gem," that is, a gem that comes from a living thing. Coral (formed from a colony of marine invertebrates) and amber (fossilized tree sap) are also organic gems. In the case of the pearl, it is produced by several species of saltwater and freshwater molluscs, soft-bodied animals protected by a hard exterior shell. But don't expect to get lucky at the dinner table — most pearl-producing varieties are not the edible types!

Molluscs include oysters, clams, mussels, snails, squid, octopus, and many other shellfish. There are over 100,000 different types, but only a few varieties produce the lovely pearls for which we long.

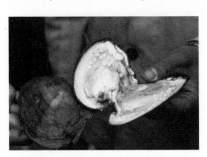

A hinged *bi-valve* freshwater mollusc.

Pearls are produced in particular varieties of *bivalve* molluscs (having *two* shells, such as mussels and oysters), but only in those with a "pearly" lining on the interior of the shell. Not all bivalves that produce "mother-of-pearl," as this shell lining is called, actually produce pearls, but only such types can produce a true pearl.

In the case of natural pearls, a tiny intruder such as a sea parasite finds its way into a mollusc's shell, and lodges itself inside. If the mollusc can't get rid of it, it begins to produce something to soothe the irritation the intruder causes; this soothing secretion is a brownish substance called *conchiolin* (kon-KY-oh-lin, "ky" as in "sky"), over which another substance is secreted, usually a whitish substance, called *nacre* (NAY-ker). The conchiolin binds the nacre together to form the pearl.

What we know as a "pearl" is the result of the buildup of layer after layer of nacre, enveloping the intruder. Nacre is the same substance that forms the lining within the shell. It is composed of microscopic *crystals* of calcium carbonate, primarily calcite and aragonite. When there are a sufficient number of layers, and when the crystals are properly aligned with each other, a *prismatic* effect is created as light travels through each layer. This prismatic effect creates a rainbow-like glow across the pearl's surface — a soft iridescence — which is referred to as the pearl's "orient." This lustrous glow and soft iridescent quality produced by the nacre is what gives a fine pearl its unique beauty and character. The thicker the nacre, and more perfectly aligned each crystal layer, the more beautiful, rare, and costly the pearl.

Parts of a mollusc.

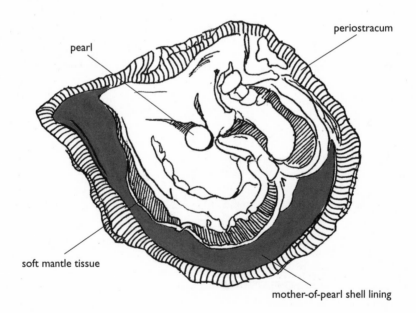

periostracum

pearl

soft mantle tissue

mother-of-pearl shell lining

A pearl is not very hard compared to other gems — 2.5-3.5 on Mohs' hardness scale — but its compact nature makes it surprisingly durable and very resistant to knocks and blows; many pearls have retained their beauty for hundreds of years, as the legendary pearls we've mentioned can attest. Once, when I was clapping furiously, the natural pearl in my ring went sailing across a convention hall, hit the wall and bounced along the floor! Luckily someone heard my shout, saw it, and retrieved it for me; I was amazed that it was not harmed at all.

Natural pearls are produced by "wild" molluscs in their native habitat, but most wild molluscs don't contain pearls. Depending upon a variety of conditions, it can take 10 years or longer for an oyster to produce a 6 millimeter pearl, and far longer for pearls of 7 or 8 millimeters. The longer the pearl remains in the mollusc, however, the more likely that its beauty will be marred, especially its surface, so large natural pearls of fine quality are especially rare. A pearl diver might dive an entire lifetime and amass only a handful of natural pearls, and of those, most of the larger pearls will not be very beautiful.

The fine pearls so much in demand — the "nacreous" variety consisting of many layers of nacre — are only produced by certain types of molluscs, or shellfish, as we mentioned earlier. Other types of shellfish can produce a pearl-like product, but few have lasting beauty or commercial value. As a child playing in the creeks of Virginia, I used to find lovely, pastel colored "pearls" in the heads of *crayfish.* My collection consisted of numerous shiny, roundish pearls, approximately 7-8 millimeters in diameter, in a rainbow of colors — pink, pale green, cream, white, and even blue. Unfortunately, in a rather short time the shine would subside, the color fade, and the pearl would eventually deteriorate and crumble. So I finally abandoned crayfish hunting and dissection!

Such products are called *calcareous concretions,* and many shellfish produce them. This is what most people find in edible oysters; they are not true pearls and most, like my "crayfish pearls," are not beautiful or durable. Sometimes people find a true pearl while eating a *freshwater mussel,* but this is a different type of mollusc than the pearl producing, saltwater type.

The largest, most beautiful pearls sought throughout history are produced by saltwater molluscs. While we refer to them as pearl-producing *oysters,* this may really be a misnomer; oysters are an edible mollusc from the family *ostreidae* and most saltwater pearls are produced by non-edible molluscs more akin to the scallop family. In this book we will refer to the saltwater pearl-producing mollusc as an "oyster," but don't be surprised if at some future date you hear them called scallops!

Today, most of the world's wild, natural pearl producing molluscs have vanished because of overfishing and pollution, so beautiful natural pearls are rarer than ever before. Some jewelers still obtain them occasionally for special clients who can appreciate and afford them (primarily from auctions, estate jewelry, and agents for private estates), but they continue to be reserved for only the privileged few.

The Pearl Market Is a Cultured Market Today

As natural pearls were becoming extinct, the Japanese were developing techniques for producing *cultured* pearls, also called *cultivated* pearls. A cultured pearl is also a *natural* product, produced by a mollusc in essentially the same way it produces a natural pearl, but with the help of science. In the cultured pearl, technicians start the process by *implanting* the object that stimulates the oyster to produce the conchiolin and nacre that results, ultimately, in the creation of the pearl.

Differences between Cultured and Natural Pearls

One way to understand the difference between a natural pearl and a cultured pearl is to think of the natural pearl as a product of the mollusc working alone, and the cultured pearl as a product of science *helping* nature. In the natural pearl, the irritating intruder that starts the whole process we discussed earlier is a very tiny intruder — often microscopic — such as a parasitic worm that bores its way through the shell into the oyster tissue; in the cultured pearl, technicians surgically implant the "intruder." In *round* saltwater and freshwater cultured pearls, the implant is normally a *round* bead, accompanied by a piece of mantle tissue; this round bead/mantle tissue implant is called the *nucleus* and these are referred to as "nucleated" cultured pearls. The mantle tissue carries the cells that start the production of conchiolin and nacre; placing it next to the round bead assures that the *bead* will be nacre-coated, hopefully becoming a nice, *round* pearl.

In most freshwater cultured pearls, the lovely irregularly-shaped pearls that resemble rice-krispies, the implants may be mantle tissue alone; these are referred to as "tissue graft" or "non-nucleated" cultured pearls. Freshwater pearls produced from mantle tissue alone are usually *not* round, but elongated and asymmetrical in shape.

The implant, whether bead and mantle tissue or mantle tissue alone, is referred to as the "nucleus" and it is the implanting of a nucleus that causes the irritation that the mollusc must soothe, thus creating the pearl. The prized round pearls so coveted today are bead-nucleated pearls, produced by saltwater oysters.

Inserting the nucleus requires a very delicate operation performed by highly skilled technicians. The nucleus is made from a *natural, organic* substance. For round, saltwater pearls, the nucleus is normally a *smooth, round sphere* made from the shell of a particular type of mollusc that lives only in the United States, in rivers and lakes fed by the Mississippi River. A different variety of shell was recently used (as an experiment) by some pearl producers in Japan and China, with disastrous results; the pearls containing these experimental nuclei began to change color in just months, and the nucleus itself — the very core of the pearl — began to deteriorate within, weakening the pearl and resulting in a *life expectancy under two years.* (If you buy pearls that begin to discolor after so short a time, return them to your jeweler immediately.)

A fine pearl requires a cultivation period of two to three years in the oyster to acquire a thick nacre coating that will give it lasting beauty. But there is a delicate interplay of numerous factors occurring within the mollusc during the cultivation period that affects the final appearance of the pearl, and the longer it remains in the mollusc, the higher the probability that certain desirable characteristics will be adversely affected, especially shape and surface perfection. Remember that *the nucleus is round and smooth* at the very start, before any nacre has begun to cover it. As the nacre coating accumulates and thickens around the sphere at its core, it can become increasingly out-of-round or misshapen, and increasingly spotted. So, a short cultivation period results in a much larger crop of *rounder* pearls with *smoother surfaces,* but with *thin nacre* and *less longevity;* a longer cultivation period results in *thicker nacre* and *longer life,* but fewer pearls with perfectly round shapes and spotless surfaces. This is why the finest round pearls are so rare, and costly.

During the cultivation period, the oysters receive constant attention and care to help assure that they will thrive and produce the best possible pearl crop. But there are no guarantees. The culturing process is very delicate and fragile, and after all of the effort that it requires, one still has little control over the final results. Pearl farmers can't control whether or not the oysters will accept or reject the nucleus after the implant procedure; they can't control the quality of the pearl the oyster produces, for each individual oyster determines the lustrousness, shape, color, surface smoothness, and so on; and they can't control or prevent the natural disasters that can destroy the oysters, their habitat, or their lustrous creations — typhoons, earthquakes, disease, or other "acts of God." The Japanese have suffered great loss as a result of the deadly "red tide." and Kobe, the pearl capital of Japan, was nearly destroyed in 1995 by one of the most serious earthquakes in modern history. Indonesian

South Sea pearl production has been plagued by repeated earthquakes as well, and the American freshwater cultured pearl harvest was severely damaged as a result of chemicals leaching into the water from a nearby state road project in which lime was being used.

Despite the best efforts of pearl producers, and the advances of science and technology, in the end it is *the oyster* and *nature* that determine whether or not there will be a pearl at all, and if so, whether or not it will be beautiful and valuable.

Left: The round, mother-of-pearl bead nucleus used to produce cultured pearls, cut and shaped from the shell of freshwater molluscs from Tennessee rivers and lakes.
Right: Cultured pearl, and cross-section showing nucleus within.

How Long Does It Take to Make a Beautiful Pearl?

In the case of natural pearls, as we mentioned, it can take many years to create a beautiful pearl. With cultured pearls, the cultivation period — the amount of time the nucleus remains in the mollusc after the implant procedure — normally ranges from about two years to six months, or less. The shorter the cultivation period, the thinner the nacre; the longer the cultivation period, the thicker the nacre. If the cultivation period is too short, the pearls will not last. Buyers must be careful not to buy pearls with nacre that is too thin.

The length of the cultivation period is a matter of serious debate today. At one time pearls remained in the oyster for much longer periods, up to five years; in the 1920s to 1940s, the cultivation period was much longer than it is today so most cultured pearls had *very thick* nacre. However, surfaces were more spotted. For cultured pearl growers today, escalating production costs and ever-present natural risks to the oyster crop are reduced by shortening the cultivation period, as are deviations in shape and imperfections across the surface of the pearl. Each pearl producer must decide how to best balance all the factors involved so that a lovely pearl is produced, at an affordable price, without unnecessary risk.

How Much of the Pearl Is Really "Pearl"?

The primary physical differences between natural and cultured pearls are related to the thickness of the actual "pearl" substance, the nacre. The thickness of the nacre affects size, shape, beauty, and how long the pearl will last.

In cultured pearls, the *size of the nucleus* dictates the *size of the pearl*; in cultured pearl production, larger pearls are produced by inserting a larger nucleus, smaller pearls by implanting a smaller nucleus. The time required to produce a large cultured pearl is essentially the same as that required to produce a smaller cultured pearl.

Implanting normally begins in January/February with harvesting in November. The largest nuclei are implanted first, to give them the advantage of a slightly longer cultivation period; the smallest are implanted last, sometimes several months later, and usually have a shorter cultivation period, but since the nucleus is smaller the *ratio* of nacre is normally still comparable to larger pearls.

While it takes several years to raise the mollusc and produce a fine cultured pearl, natural pearls take *many* years, even for very small pearls. With natural pearls, the pearl is essentially all nacre, with no nucleus at its core. The process that creates the natural pearl is usually started by a very small intruder, so the size of the pearl is an indication of the number of years the pearl has been in the mollusc rather than the size of an implant. Small natural pearls have normally been in the mollusc for a shorter time; larger pearls a much longer time.

Large natural pearls of fine quality are among the rarest of earth's treasures. Keep in mind that among all the pearl-producing molluscs, only a very small percentage ever experience that unique set of natural circumstances that results in the creation of the pearl. Furthermore, in nature there are more variables affecting the quality and beauty of the pearl — not all natural pearls are of fine quality; not all are beautiful and desirable. The larger the pearl, the less likely it will be fine and beautiful; as in cultured pearls, the longer the pearl remains in the mollusc, the greater the likelihood that there will be defects in its shape, surface perfection, nacre crystallization, and so on. And, last but not least, natural pearl-producing molluscs have never been conveniently located for easy access, and diving for natural pearls has always been very perilous, often ending in death. Divers have spent entire lifetimes diving for pearls, to end up with little more than a handful of small pearls for their work. Among all the known natural pearls, including famous historical pearls, fine large pearls are few and far between.

Diving for natural pearls continues today in various parts of the world, but for the most part, the oyster beds known for fine natural pearls have been killed by pollution. Discovering so rare a treasure as a large, fine, natural pearl holds a powerful allure to some, but for most the discovery will never be more than a dream.

Some very fine jewelry firms still seek and acquire fine natural pearls, but they are even rarer today than ever before. A very fine 15 millimeter round cultured pearl is not as rare as the natural, but it is still a costly treasure. Whether cultured or natural, the larger the pearl, the rarer and costlier.

In cultured pearls, cultivators insert several different size nuclei into molluscs, producing a variety of pearl sizes at harvest. At first glance this might suggest that it is easy to get any size pearl the grower wishes, including large sizes, but this is not the case. Only a very small percentage ever experience the unique set of circumstances that results in the creation of a beautiful, fine quality pearl, and, *as the size of the nucleus increases, the quantity of fine quality pearls actually harvested decreases.* As the size of the nucleus increases, fewer molluscs survive the implant operation, and more molluscs reject the nucleus, so fewer pearls are actually harvested. Furthermore, the larger the nucleus, the more difficult it becomes for the mollusc to produce a pearl with fine color, luster, surface perfection and shape. This means there are *fewer* pearls actually harvested, and far fewer *fine* pearls. This is why larger cultured pearls of fine quality are rarer, and why they cost so much more than comparable smaller cultured pearls.

Differences You Can See — Differences You Can't See

The thickness of the nacre affects size, shape, beauty, and how long the pearl will last. The natural pearl is all pearl, or all nacre, while most cultured pearls consists of a nucleus *coated* with nacre. The thicker the nacre coating on the cultured pearl, the more beautiful it will be.

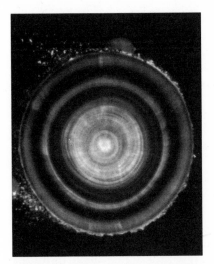 

Left: Natural pearl in cross section, showing concentric rings of nacre.
Right: Cultured pearl in cross section, showing large nucleus.

Very few people can *see* any difference between a very fine cultured pearl *with thick nacre* and a very fine natural pearl. Both will exhibit a rich, deep, intense lustrousness accentuated by a beautiful, soft iridescent "play of color" — sometimes referred to as "orient" — that can be seen moving across the surface of the pearl as it moves in the light.

Generally speaking, however, there are some visual clues that might suggest natural or cultured:

• *Matching.* Because of their scarcity and limited supply, *matching* of natural pearls was often ignored, especially as the size increased, so necklaces often contain pearls with marked differences in size, color, and shape.

• *Color.* In terms of color, natural pearls are usually *creamier* than today's finest cultured pearls.

• *Shape.* In terms of shape, natural pearls are rarely truly "round," and necklaces often seem to contain pearls that seem *out-of-round* to today's pearl buyer.

"Cultured" Tastes
May Not Recognize Natural Treasures!

Finding an appreciative buyer for such a rare beauty as a strand of natural pearls may be rarer than the pearls themselves. The reason for this isn't difficult to understand if you think about it for a moment. There is really nothing in nature that is truly "perfect," a fact that, where gems are concerned, was more fully appreciated and accepted in days gone by. Natural pearls are just that, natural. As such, differences abound, and given their rarity to begin with, there was often no choice about what was available to use. With cultured pearls there are much larger quantities of pearls from which to choose, so it is easier to find and carefully match them.

Since cultured pearls now dominate the market, we have come to expect a certain "look" in pearls, a look rarely found in natural pearls — uniformity, whiteness, roundness, *and much larger sizes than are normally seen in natural pearls.* Ironically, this has had a negative impact on natural pearls. While much rarer than cultured pearls, a strand of "small" natural pearls will have a perceived value of much *less* than a larger strand of cultured pearls.

I recently witnessed an example of this. I saw a magnificent natural pearl necklace containing exceptionally fine, well matched, bright, lustrous, round pearls. This very rare necklace was about 34 inches long and contained pearls ranging from over 6.7 millimeters to just under 7.65 millimeters (most being over 7 millimeters), giving the impression of a uniform necklace — another rarity in natural pearls of this size, length and quality.

This necklace represents one of nature's rarest treasures. For natural pearls, the pearls were very large. Compared to cultured pearls, however, they were small. At $65,000, the price was not small! Today, it is difficult to sell such a necklace because few will guess what it is, or appreciate its importance.

Before this era of cultured pearls, such a necklace would have found an immediate home in some illustrious setting, and been treasured and cherished by its owner. As it is today, it is so fine — so white and so well matched — that ironically, it could be confused with a fine *cultured* pearl necklace, and perceived to have a much lower value ($1/10$ of what it is really worth)! While people may have some idea of how much a large, "important" cultured pearl necklace might cost, very few understand the value represented in a natural pearl necklace, especially one which appears to be so modest in size. And let's face it, most buyers spending a large sum on a piece of jewelry want others to recognize its value. Only a connoisseur would pay such a price for a necklace of this size, for a necklace that could be confused with a cultured pearl necklace of much less value; only a connoisseur could appreciate it for the priceless, rare and magnificent *natural* treasure that it is. I've never seen another natural pearl necklace of this length that was comparable in terms of overall quality, matching, and size. Nor can I imagine when or where another of comparable beauty might be found.

Absence of Uniformity
May Hint at Natural Treasure

In a market so totally dominated by cultured pearls, we've come to expect precise matching in pearl strands, and perfection of shape and surface smoothness in individual pearls; pearls that aren't "perfect" or well matched are assumed to be "poor quality" cultured pearls. As a result, *natural* pearls are sometimes ignored because they aren't recognized for what they are. I recently acquired a wonderful triple-strand *natural pearl necklace* at auction, for the price of a poor quality cultured pearl necklace! It was described in the catalogue as a "cultured" pearl necklace, and, because the pearls weren't especially large (they ranged from approximately 4.5 to 7 millimeters in diameter), no one thought the necklace warranted any special testing. I remember one of the jewelry department staff people saying subsequently that she couldn't understand why it mattered very much to me that they turned out to be natural because, after all, they weren't very "important." She was referring to their size. Perhaps they were not very important to her, but to me they are very special, and exhibit a character rarely seen in cultured pearls. I wear them with great pleasure, knowing how rare they truly are. And, I must add, I'm grateful to cultured pearl marketers for creating this "cultured pearl market" in which someone like me might be able to acquire such a rare *natural* treasure! Every time I wear it I think about how, in ages past, owning a necklace such as this would have been a possibility only among the wealthiest and most powerful — and I do wonder just who might have owned these!

Small natural pearl necklaces and other pieces of jewelry with small natural pearls are often ignored today at auctions or estate sales, and the absence of uniformity is often the first visible clue. So, while the finest natural pearls and natural pearl necklaces can command stellar prices, many smaller natural pearls can now be acquired at auction and from private estates at very attractive prices. If the idea of owning a rare natural pearl necklace appeals to you, remember that uniformity in a strand is *rarely* the case, and one indicator of what you might have may well be the *absence of uniformity!*

A *natural* pearl necklace with fine ruby and diamond clasp, a gift to Empress Eugénie from her husband Napoleon III. Note the irregularity in the size and shape of the pearls. There are also noticeable differences in color.

How to Tell the Natural from the Cultured Pearl

Appreciation for natural pearls is increasing as people learn more about them and how they compare to cultured pearls, and as interest in heirloom jewelry, antiques and estate pieces increases. Strengthening prices for natural pearls at auction and among fine estate dealers seems to indicate that they are a collectible with a lustrous future. Here is how one can determine whether a pearl is cultured or natural:

- **Examine the drill hole.** If a pearl has been drilled, a jeweler or gemologist can usually identify a cultured pearl very easily. By examining several pearls, looking into the drill hole carefully with a loupe (a jeweler's special magnifying lens), the line of demarcation between the mother-of-pearl nucleus and the layer of conchiolin may be visible, sometimes appearing as a darker line. It may not be visible in all pearls, and you may only see a portion of the line in a given pearl. If the strand is tightly knotted (as in a newly strung necklace), you may have to try several pearls before finding enough space between the pearl and knot to be able to use the loupe. When this darker area is visible, you can be sure you have a cultured pearl. NOTE: Many cultured pearls have been bleached to remove the brownish conchiolin line. Also, it won't be seen in cultured pearls with extremely thick nacre. When you can't see this brownish layer, you must test further.

  The size of the drill hole is sometimes an important indicator. Very small drill holes may indicate "natural." Since natural pearls are valued in part by weight, great care was taken to keep the hole as small as possible to minimize loss of weight, and maintain maximum value.

- **Examine with an ultraviolet lamp, using long-wave ultraviolet radiation** (an inexpensive "black light" is all you need). Examination with ultraviolet light is often helpful when examining pearls that don't show any line of demarcation, when it's difficult to view the drill hole, or in cases where the pearl is undrilled. It can be especially useful with necklaces or bracelets. When examined under ultraviolet light, cultured pearls normally have a strong, milky, bluish-white appearance. In the case of cultured pearl strands, this response will be uniform throughout; in a natural strand, there will be variations from pearl to pearl in the intensity of color seen. Natural pearls often appear a tan or yellowish color when viewed under ultraviolet light.

- **Examine with a strong penlight or fiber optic light.** View the pearl from several different directions while holding a strong light in direct contact with it, slowly moving it around the pearl's surface without losing contact. If viewed in this manner, it is sometimes possible to see dark, parallel lines from the mother-of-pearl nucleus showing through the nacre (especially in cultured pearls with very thin nacre). These dark, parallel lines always indicate cultured.

With a strong light, viewed in this way, you might also notice some orangey-colored, irregularly shaped spots, some large and some small. This is an indication of cultured pearls.

- **X-ray examination.** Cultured pearls can often be identified as cultured by the above tests. However, such tests are inconclusive on undrilled pearls and cultured pearls with extremely thick nacre such as South Sea cultured pearls or American freshwater cultured pearls. In these cases, pearls must be x-rayed.

Cross-section of cultured pearl showing *parallel banding* of the nucleus. In poor quality, thin-nacre pearls, this parallel banding can sometimes be seen when the pearl is examined in strong light.

If you think you might have a strand of natural pearls but aren't sure, submit them to a reliable gem testing laboratory for documentation. Natural pearls must be x-rayed to confirm authenticity. If you are buying pearls represented to be natural, make sure there is an accompanying identification report from a reliable lab, or make the sale contingent upon getting one. Always be sure to have proper documentation, no matter how old the piece, who the owner is, or how wealthy. NOTE: *Be sure to have an experienced gem-testing laboratory perform the tests and make the determination. I know of people who have made costly mistakes based on the erroneous reading of an x-ray taken by a dentist or friend.*

Cultured versus Imitation Pearls

Today when jewelers speak of "genuine" or "real" pearls, they mean *cultured* pearls. This is what you see in jewelry stores, and this is what we will be covering, unless otherwise indicated, in this book. According to the United States' *Federal Trade Commission Guidelines,* however, the terms "real" and "genuine" can be used only for *natural* pearls unless followed immediately by the term "cultured," and the term "cultured" *immediately preceding the word pearl, "and with equal conspicuity."*

How Do Imitation Pearls Differ from Cultured?

Natural pearls and cultured pearls are produced in rivers, lakes, and bays by living molluscs and can be very similar in appearance. Imitation pearls — also called "faux," "simulated," and most recently, "semi-cultured" — are not created by any living creature. They should not be referred to in any way as genuine or cultured. Imitation pearls have never seen the inside of a mollusc. They are entirely artificial, made from round glass, plastic, or mother-of-pearl beads dipped in a bath of ground fish scales and lacquer (called *pearlessence*), or one of the new plastic substances. The difference can usually be seen right away when compared side by side. One of the most obvious differences is in the luster. Give it the LUSTER TEST; the cultured pearl will have a depth of luster that the fake cannot duplicate. The fake usually has a surface "shine" but no inner "glow." Look at a fine cultured pearl and an imitation pearl side by side (away from direct light) and notice the difference.

Use the "Tooth Test" to Spot the Fake

There are some fine imitations today that can be very convincing. Some have actually been mistaken for fine cultured pearls. An easy, reliable test in most cases is the "tooth test." Run the pearl gently along the edge of your teeth (the upper teeth are more sensitive, and also be aware that the test won't work with false teeth). The genuine pearl will have a mildly abrasive or gritty feel (think of the gritty feeling of sand at the seaside — real pearls come from the sea), while the imitation will be slippery smooth (like the con artist, slippery smooth signifies a fake!). Try this test on pearls you know are genuine, and then on known imitations to get a feel for the difference. You'll never forget it!

The tooth test may be unreliable for amateurs when applied to the imitation "Majorica" pearl, however. Although to the trained eye they have a very different look from cultured pearls, this is an imitation pearl which might be mistaken for genuine. Close examination of the surface under magnification will reveal a fine "pinpoint" surface that is very different from the smooth surface of a cultured or natural pearl. An experienced jeweler or gemologist can quickly and easily identify the Majorica for you.

Chapter 4

Different Types of Pearls:
A Pearl for Every Mood

There has never been a period in history when pearls were not in vogue. And today is no exception. They go well with any style, in any place; they can be worn from morning to evening; they look smart and attractive with sportswear, add an "executive" touch to the business suit, or add elegance to even the most glamorous evening gown.

Today when one mentions "pearls" many different images might come to mind. There are many more types of pearls available today than ever before. They offer a variety of colors, shapes, and sizes, and a wide range in price. Depending upon what catches your fancy, you can spend under $100, or over $1,000,000!

There are simple pearls for the "sweet sixteen"; there are romantic pearls to add magic to the wedding day; there are classic pearls for the executive; there are one-of-a-kind pearls for the creative individualist; there are "important" pearls to mark an important milestone. Like diamonds, rubies, emeralds and sapphires, there is a pearl for every age, every occasion, every personal style, and every budget.

With so many possibilities, just knowing where to begin can be overwhelming. But it doesn't have to be. The key is in knowing what types are available, how they compare to each other, and how to recognize quality differences.

The variety available today results from the use of different types of oysters, the physical environment in which they live, and varying cultivation techniques used by the producers. They are generally classified as *saltwater* cultured pearls or *freshwater* cultured pearls, and divided into the *white* category, which includes shades from pink-white to silver-white to creamy-white and yellow-white, and the *fancy color* category, the best known of which are the natural color black cultured pearls and the deep yellows and golden cultured pearls. They are also classified as *round* or *baroque*. A baroque pearl is, technically, any pearl that is not round; within the baroque category, pearls are also classified as *symmetrical* or *asymmetrical*. Symmetrical baroque pearls can be very costly (some comparable to round pearls) while asymmetrical baroques are normally much more affordable than round cultured pearls.

Cultured pearls offer wide variety in color, shape and size.

Here we will discuss both in a general way. In Chapter 8 we will explore the leading pearl producing nations of the world, and compare their pearls.

Saltwater Cultured Pearls

Cultured saltwater, or "sea" pearls, are grown today by pearl-producing oysters in several parts of the world, including Australia, China, French Polynesia, Indonesia, Japan, Korea, and the Philippines. Among the best-known are the Japanese "Akoya" (the classic round, white pearl), the larger "South Sea pearl," and the naturally black Tahitian pearl.

In the 1950s, cultured pearls meant Japanese "Akoya" pearls, and Mikimoto owned most of the oyster beds — about 12,000,000 oysters — accounting for about 75% of the world's supply of cultured pearls. Since the 1960s, however, the production of cultured pearls began to extend to other pearl farmers in Japan, and to other parts of the world.

Classic round, white, cultured pearl known as the Akoya type, set in award-winning brooch by M. Kondo.

While the basic pearl-producing process is the same in a saltwater or freshwater mollusc, in the case of round cultured pearls there is one significant difference; the production of most freshwater pearls, such as the "rice-krispie" type, requires the insertion of a piece of mantle tissue alone, while the production of round cultured pearls requires the insertion of a round "bead" nucleus in addition to the piece of mantle tissue. Following the surgical implant of the nucleus, many will either reject the implant or die; of those remaining, more will die before harvest. Only 30% to 35% of the original group of oysters will actually produce a pearl. Only a very small fraction of the pearls produced will be fine quality.

Saltwater cultured pearls command higher prices than freshwater cultured pearls. As you can imagine, the costs and the risks involved in producing saltwater cultured pearls are much greater. They are much costlier to produce than most freshwater pearls, although American freshwater cultured pearls are also very expensive to produce (see Chapter 8). Higher costs are incurred just to obtain the shell from which the round, mother-of-pearl nuclei are fashioned, and to make them; higher labor costs are incurred for skilled technicians to perform the implant surgery; higher costs are incurred because a much greater number of "spat" (baby oysters) must be collected and raised to insure an adequate supply of mature oysters for cultivation, and because a much greater number of oysters is required for a good yield; and so on.

The most important reason for the cost difference, however, is that an individual saltwater oyster normally can produce only one or two sizeable pearls at a time. In American freshwater cultured pearl production, only one to five can be produced at a time. By comparison, in China or Japan, *a single freshwater mussel can produce 15-20 pearls at a time, or more.*

Freshwater Pearls

Freshwater cultured pearls are grown in freshwater rather than saltwater, in mussels that live in lakes and rivers. One of the best known freshwater pearls is the *Biwa* pearl (named after Lake Biwa in Japan), which is one of the finest and most beautiful of the freshwater pearls. It often occurs in oval, barrel, and coin shapes. Although the term "Biwa" should be used only for pearls from Lake Biwa, it is often used indiscriminately to refer to *any* freshwater pearl; since Lake Biwa once produced almost all of the fine freshwater pearls, it has become a generic label for almost all freshwater pearls. Unfortunately, Lake Biwa production now has virtually ceased, and Chinese freshwater cultured pearls are being sent to Japan and sold as "Biwa."

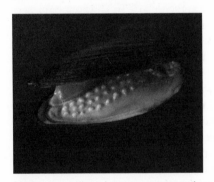

Freshwater mollusc showing approximately 30 freshwater pearls within. After harvesting, this mollusc will be returned to the water to produce another pearl crop.

Necklace using rare Lake Biwa "X" pearls.

Freshwater cultured pearls are now grown in many countries. The leading producers include the United States, Japan, and China. Common mussel-type molluscs are used. The process used to produce most freshwater pearls doesn't require a shell nucleus; tissue grafting techniques are used instead, which facilitates mass production. The mollusc is also larger than that used to produce Akoya pearls. As a result, an individual mollusc can produce as many as 20 to 30 pearls at a time, or more. The pearls produced in this manner are normally small and very inexpensive. Using only mantle tissue, however, they are essentially all nacre, and top quality freshwater pearls are very lovely and offer very good value for the money. They occur in a wide range of colors and shapes, the most familiar having a long, narrow, rice-shaped outline, generally with a wrinkled surface, although the surface can be very smooth. They can have high luster or low, depending upon quality. Japan and China are the leading producers of this type of freshwater cultured pearl.

The look of freshwater cultured pearls is changing, however. Very lovely *round* freshwater cultured pearls are also being produced today. These require more sophisticated production techniques, including an implant procedure. The exact technique being used has not been disclosed, but may involve the use of a *round* implant, possibly fashioned from the inexpensive, all-nacre tissue-nucleated pearl that is so abundant. The result is a *round, cultured* pearl that is essentially *all nacre*! China is the primary source of these lovely pearls (see Chapter 8), but most are under 6 millimeters in size. We can also expect to see quantities of round *American* freshwater cultured pearls in the near future. Round freshwater pearls are more expensive than other types of freshwater cultured pearls, but normally much less expensive than round, saltwater pearls.

Some of the world's most prized — and most beautiful — pearls are *natural* freshwater pearls. These are very expensive and can compare to the price of natural saltwater pearls. Frequently whiter than the natural saltwater pearl, and often with a more intense luster, these are the pearls that were so cherished by the Romans — pearls found in the rivers of the European countries they conquered. The only reason the Roman legions ever ventured into England, or so it is rumored, was to search for the rare and beautiful *pink* freshwater pearls found in Scotland!

Cultured freshwater pearls also occur in interesting shapes, as do the natural; in fact, natural "angel-wing" pearls from the Mississippi River and other nearby rivers and lakes are very collectible. Cultured pearl producers are also culturing freshwater pearls in special shapes such as crosses, bars, and coins. These are referred to as *fancy* shapes.

Freshwater pearls occur in a wide range of colors — a much wider variety than round, saltwater pearls — which gives them a special allure. Colors include light, medium, and dark orange, lavender, purple, violet, blue, rose, and gray. Large natural freshwater pearls in unusual colors can be *very* expensive. Freshwater pearls may also be dyed. When buying freshwater pearls, be sure to ask if the color is natural.

Another interesting feature of freshwater pearls is that they can be worn singly or grouped in alternating colors, either hanging straight or twisted for a distinctive effect. In addition to the versatility offered by the many color options, the lower cost of most freshwater pearls (with the exception of round) makes it possible to buy many strands and create an almost endless variety of looks.

American Freshwater Cultured Pearls — Distinctly American

There are no other pearls being produced at this time anywhere in the world that resemble the American freshwater *cultured* pearl. They are not at all the typical round, white pearls we think of when we think of pearls. They have a look entirely their own, a result of being produced by very different methods, in a variety of mollusc that lives only in American rivers and lakes. Tennessee is the primary source of these American beauties as well as the source of the shell used to make the mother-of-pearl beads for nucleating cultured pearls in all other parts of the world.

American freshwater cultured pearls are produced by very unconventional freshwater culturing techniques which took years to develop. The first difference, and most important, is that *a mother-of-pearl bead nucleus is implanted, as in saltwater cultured pearl production.* Using a freshwater mollusc, however, combined with unconventional placement of the nucleus, results in a pearl with a very different appearance from other cultured pearls

To produce American freshwater cultured pearls the nucleus is left inside the mollusc for a much longer time than is the case with other cultured pearls — from *three to five years,* compared to less than 12 months in most saltwater cultivation — giving them

An array of American freshwater cultured pearls including "domé®," sticks, bars, coins, marquises and navettes.

a much thicker nacre than is normally found in cultured pearls, and a lustrousness and orient to which only the very finest cultured saltwater pearls, and natural pearls, can compare.

Another significant difference is that *the American freshwater cultured pearl is never dyed, bleached, or enhanced* (see Chapter 6). This creates a pearl that in many ways more closely resembles the natural pearl than other types of cultured pearls, including its longevity; the beauty of American freshwater cultured pearls will last longer than most cultured saltwater pearls now being produced. Of course, it also means, as with natural pearls, that there are marked differences in color, shape, and surface perfection, so matching is more difficult. These pearls are only for those who enjoy, appreciate and value the subtle differences nature places in all her creations.

Although much more affordable than saltwater cultured pearls, the cost is higher than for most other freshwater cultured pearls. American freshwater cultured pearls occur in a variety of distinctive shapes not seen in other types of pearls — coin shapes, bars, marquises, ovals, and round "domés®" that resemble mabé pearls (see below).

Distinctive jewelry using American freshwater cultured pearls: a ring and brooch using the domé® pearl; a pendant highlighting a "navette" shaped pearl as the body of a swordfish.

Baroque Pearls

The rarest pearls are *round* pearls, and round pearls in fine quality are very costly. A *baroque* pearl, technically, is any pearl that is *not* round and has an interesting irregular shape. Baroque pearls shouldn't be confused with pearls that are simply "out-of-round" (this is the least desirable shape). They should have a distinctive enough shape to be interesting and attractive. Baroque pearls can be produced by both saltwater and freshwater molluscs, and can be natural or cultured. They have a distinctive appeal because of their very beautiful tints of color and iridescent flashes, which are the result of "pools" of nacre (where the baroque shape creates an area in which the nacre can collect, and is deeper than along other parts of the pearl). Baroque pearls, with their distinctive irregular shapes, are more common than round pearls, which makes them more affordable, but they can make beautiful jewelry creations.

Top left: A distinctive necklace highlighting a magnificent Australian South Sea baroque pearl.
Top right: Fine *symmetrical* pear-shape pearls, and very affordable irregularly shaped "teardrop" baroques.
Bottom left: An interesting baroque pearl resembling a roasting chicken!
Bottom right: Button pearl

Symmetrical Pearls

A symmetrical pearl is one that is not round, but which has a beautiful, symmetrical shape, such as "teardrop" or "oval." While they may be in the "baroque" class (since they are not round), they are rare, and, depending upon the shape and how perfect it is, a matched pair can be as costly as the roundest of pearls, or even more costly.

Button pearls are a type of symmetrical pearl produced *naturally* by both saltwater and freshwater molluscs. *Cultured* button pearls are produced primarily by saltwater oysters, but we are beginning to see some freshwater cultured button pearls from China. They are sought for their very distinctive and interesting shape: they have a flattish bottom and rounded top often resembling a "squash" or "cap" similar to that worn by the Catholic Pope. They make lovely earrings and rings. They are less expensive than the finest round pearls, but depending upon the shape, size, and other factors, can still be expensive.

Types of Saltwater and Freshwater Pearls

Mabé Pearls

A mabé (MAH-bee or mah-BAY) pearl is a dome-shaped pearl available in a variety of shapes, the most common being round or pear shapes. These pearls are produced very inexpensively, but they provide a very large, attractive look at affordable prices, compared to other pearls of comparable size. They are more fragile than other pearls and should be worn and handled with care.

The mabé is an *assembled* pearl produced by placing a hemisphere-shaped piece of plastic against the side of the shell interior. The oyster then produces a nacre coating over the plastic. The resulting "pearl" is cut from the shell, and the plastic removed (since the nacre won't adhere to the plastic). The remaining hollow nacre "blister" is

Mabé pearls in assorted shapes and sizes.

then *filled* with epoxy, following which a mother-of-pearl backing is attached. These pearls are not as durable as solid "blister" pearls (see below), so some extra care should be taken when handling or wearing them. Be sure to wrap them in a soft cloth, and separate them from other jewelry, to protect them from getting scratched.

It is especially important when selecting mabé pearls to select pearls with a *thick nacre* layer. This is usually indicated by the pearl's lustrousness — the presence of a soft iridescence and high luster usually indicates a thicker nacre; a chalky quality usually indicates very thin nacre. *With mabé pearls, the thinner the nacre the more*

FRAGILE the pearl — if the nacre is too thin, mabé pearls can crack or peel easily. They are especially popular for earrings and rings, but since they are more fragile than other pearls, we don't recommend them for rings.

Solid Blister Pearls

The solid "blister" pearl — such as the American domé® — is a dome-shaped pearl similar to a mabé but *not* assembled. This type of pearl is cultivated in freshwater lakes in Tennessee. It's available in several shapes, and has a distinctive look created by a mother-of-pearl border, retained from the shell lining when the pearl is removed. These pearls have an unusually high luster and a lovely iridescent play-of-color across the surface. They are more expensive than mabé pearls, but more durable.

Prizewinning brooch by Ellen Bear, centering domé® pearl.

Seed Pearls and Keshi Pearls

Seed pearls are very tiny, round, natural pearls, usually under two millimeters in size. They are rare today, but often seen in antique jewelry. They are sometimes cut in half (see *half pearls* below) to create a larger supply for a particular jewelry creation, or to remove blemishes or a misshapen side; these are much less expensive than full seed pearls. Seed pearls can be produced by both freshwater and saltwater molluscs.

Keshi pearls, also called "chance" pearls, are interesting baroque pearls accidentally produced in saltwater oysters used for cultured pearl production. Sometimes an oyster rejects its bead implant, but particles of the accompanying mantle tissue used alongside the bead remain; these particles of mantle tissue stimulate the production of nacre, resulting in the wonderful, interesting pearls we know as "keshi." They are unusual because, like natural pearls, they are essentially *all nacre*, and all natural. There is even some heated debate regarding whether or not they should technically be called natural pearls. Whatever you call them, they are comparable in every way to natural baroque pearls.

Japanese keshi are usually very small. The word "keshi" actually comes from the Japanese word meaning a tiny particle, and was used to refer to "poppy" pearls, a fitting image for the strands of minuscule pearls they describe, very tiny pearls that might be confused with natural seed pearls. At one time it was not unusual to see necklaces comprised of 20, 50, or as many as 100 strands of these tiny pearls strung together, the strands being so delicate they look like silken threads.

The keshi pearl now attracting the attention of collectors, however, is the South Sea variety, which is much larger, 8-10 millimeters and up. Virtually always baroque in shape, they offer a variety of unusual shapes, often oblong, and lend themselves to very distinctive jewelry creations. They occur in virtually all shades of color, from silvery-white to cream, gray to black, yellow to gold, even mauve and lilac tones.

Seed pearl necklace from period of Louis XVI, containing over 125,000 seed pearls.

One of the most striking characteristics of the South Sea keshi is its very intense luster and iridescence, far greater than what is normally seen in even the finest round cultured pearls.

They are very popular in Europe and the Middle East. For Moslems, they are particularly desirable because, like natural pearls, they are an all-natural creation, and by comparison to the cost of natural pearls, very affordable.

But keshi pearls are disappearing. Japanese and South Sea pearl producers are trying to reduce the number of keshi pearls being produced because the production of keshi creates a costly problem. As nature would have it, the oyster can only produce a certain amount of nacre; if keshi are consuming nacre, that leaves less for the *cultured* pearl being produced simultaneously within the same oyster. This means that the more keshi pearls, the fewer fine, round cultured pearls. As the cultured pearl growers succeed in reducing the number of these "chance" pearls, fewer keshi will be available. Predictions are that they will become more scarce in the years ahead, which is sparking serious attention from connoisseurs. If you yearn to own a keshi necklace one day, don't wait. These exquisite, all-nacre pearls may one day be a "thing of the past."

Ringed or Circlé Pearls

When a concentric ring encircles the surface of a pearl, we say it is "ringed" or "circled"; this is a type of surface characteristic that can occur on any variety of pearl. When a pearl exhibits *numerous* concentric rings from top to bottom, however, it creates a very interesting and distinctive looking pearl. Usually off-round or baroque in shape, and much less expensive than round pearls or symmetrical baroques, these "ringed" or "circlé" pearls have a special allure and are being used increasingly in jewelry — especially those from the South Pacific occurring in shades of white, gray to black, and aubergine. Artistic designers find circlé pearls an exciting choice for distinctive and dramatic creations.

White South Sea cultured "ringed" or "circlé" pearls

Half-Pearls

Half-pearls (do not confuse with mabé pearls, previously discussed) are usually small pearls (2-3 millimeter) that have been cut in half to use for border decoration, as in a continuous row of pearls surrounding a cameo or center stone. They are inexpensive, but create a lovely effect.

Three-Quarter Pearls

Three-quarter pearls are pearls that are not fully round, but *give the impression of being round.* They can be natural or cultured, freshwater or saltwater. When mounted, it may be difficult to know for sure whether you have a fully round or ¾ pearl because they are often mounted in cups to conceal the bottom and create the illusion of a fully round pearl.

A three-quarter pearl can be one of two things: a three-quarter solid cultured blister pearl, grown on the side of the interior of the shell using a nucleus that is only ¾ round (it has one flat side, which is placed against the mollusc shell, similar to the mabé, but containing a mother-of-pearl nucleus so it is solid, not hollow); or, a full round cultured pearl that has had a portion cut away to eliminate a blemish or imperfect shape. As with other cultured pearls, they occur in a range of colors and sizes — usually 8-15 millimeters — and exhibit varying degrees of lustrousness. They are much less expensive than comparable round pearls, but make an attractive alternative for those who want a larger pearl than they might otherwise be able to afford in a true round pearl.

NOTE: Be suspicious of any attractively priced large pearl *set in a cup*; it may contain a three-quarter pearl. These are frequently used in earrings.

After distinguishing between saltwater and freshwater pearls, the major categories into which cultured pearls are divided are "Akoya," "South Sea," and "Black" (or "dark") pearls. There are "Akoya" button pearls, for example, and "South Sea" keshi. And so on.

Akoya Pearls

This is the pearl that comes to mind the moment anyone mentions "pearl" — lustrous, round, white pearls. The finest Akoyas, originally produced in Japan, are more perfectly round than most other pearls and have the highest luster, which makes them especially desirable. Unfortunately, for those who prefer very large pearls, they rarely

Very fine Akoya pearls

exceed 10 millimeters in diameter, and when they do, they command exceptionally high prices. In addition to Japan, China is now a major producer of Akoyas.

South Sea Pearls

These pearls are the very large, regal white pearls often called the "queen" of cultured pearls. They are produced by a particular type of unusually large saltwater oyster, the *Pinctada maxima*. Today, all pearls produced by this oyster are referred to as "South Sea" pearls. Most are now cultivated in the waters off Australia, Indonesia, and the Philippines, although Burma was once one of the most important producers of South Sea pearls.

The oyster producing this type of pearl is much larger than the Japanese oyster; many reach a foot or more in diameter. At this time the oysters used are a *wild* species that is rare and the supply for cultivation is never certain (commercial spawning which is used in other types of pearl production has not yet been very successful); this is one reason fine South Sea pearls are so rare and expensive. South Sea pearls usually start at 10 millimeters in size, and go up from there. Pearls from 11 to 14 millimeters are the average. Pearls over 16 millimeters are considered very large. South Sea pearls are cultivated for longer periods and have much thicker nacre coatings than other pearls. This means they are often less perfectly round and more spotted than their smaller Japanese counterpart, but they are very beautiful and very expensive. The rarest, most expensive color is a warm pinkish white, but the silvery-white is perhaps more in demand and also very expensive. Yellow-whites also exist, but these are the least popular and sell for much less. "Fancy" intense yellows (truly rich yellow not in any way to be confused with off-white or yellow-white) and a wide variety of hues including many "golden" tones, are now in great demand. South Sea pearls are rare in fine qualities, and more expensive than most other pearls, but they have the longest life expectancy of any cultured pearl.

Burmese Pearls

Burma once produced the rarest, finest, and most valuable "South Sea" pearls in the world. The best Burmese possess an exceptionally high "silky" luster, unmatched by any other South Sea pearl, and a fine pink-white color. In recent years the quality of Burmese pearls has been deteriorating, however, because of a complicated political situation reducing availability of skilled technicians and disrupting quality control. Very few fine Burmese pearls are produced today; most are indistinguishable from other "South Sea" pearls and often are mixed in with them when sold.

Black Pearls

Black cultured pearls are large pearls occurring *naturally* in a range of colors from gray to black, normally in sizes over 8 millimeters, and averaging 11-12 millimeters. In very rare cases they have been known to exceed 20 millimeters. Technically a "South Sea" pearl, it is cultivated by a special variety of the *Pinctada* oyster, in lagoons in the South Pacific. Fine black pearls are rare and costly, and should not be confused with artificially colored black pearls. Tahiti is the leading producer of top quality black cultured pearls, followed by the Cook Islands and other islands of French Polynesia.

The "Abalone Pearl" and the "Conch Pearl" — Two Unique Gems from the Deep

Pearls produced by nacreous pearl-producing saltwater oysters and freshwater mussels are the focus of this book, but there are two unusual types of "pearls" that are highly prized and should be mentioned: the *abalone pearl* (pronounced "ab-uh-loh-nee") and the *conch pearl* (pronounced "konk").

Abalone Pearls

The abalone pearl is one of the most beautiful and unusual of all pearls. It is also one of the rarest. Unlike other saltwater pearls, this pearl is produced by a mollusc you do eat — it is the same abalone served in restaurants! In fact, the demand for the meat of the abalone has resulted in a serious depletion of abalone mussels and increased rarity of the abalone pearl.

The abalone produces an exquisitely colored and highly iridescent nacre and mother-of-pearl shell lining that has long been prized for inlay and shell jewelry. Like their shells, abalone pearls are vividly colored and highly iridescent.

It is a true *nacreous* pearl (consisting of many concentric layers of nacre), but it is not produced by a bivalve mollusc; it is produced by an ear-shaped *univalve* mollusc (one with a single shell, such as a snail). If one's definition of "pearl" requires that it be produced by a bivalve sea creature, then the abalone is not, technically speaking, a true pearl. On the other hand, if the deciding factor is that the beauty — the lovely luster and iridescence — result from alternating layers of *nacre*, then there can be no question that the abalone *is* a true pearl. Whatever the criteria, abalone pearls are rare and beautiful gems, especially sought after by top designers and connoisseurs around the world.

Most abalone pearls are *natural* pearls, for which there is a rapidly growing "collector" market. Many have been found in abalone off the Pacific coast of the United States. They are also found in Japan, New Zealand and Korea. We are just beginning to see a *cultured* abalone pearl market as well, with research and production underway in the United States, Japan, Korea, and New Zealand (see color section).

At this time production of cultured abalone is limited to mabé pearls (see *mabé pearls* above).

Each natural abalone pearl is unique in appearance. There are 96 known species of abalone, widely varying in shell color, size and rate of growth. These differences are reflected in the color, size and shape of the pearls produced, and account for the distinctive individuality of each abalone pearl.

The colors of the abalone pearl are rich and exotic, ranging from a metallic silvery color to steel black, cream, golden, pink and silvery-green, all with pronounced highlights of pink or magenta. The rarest and most highly prized offer rich peacock blue and green hues.

Shape is another distinguishing characteristic of natural abalone pearls. Mostly baroque, their shapes can be quite striking and this adds to their allure. Some are shaped like elongated spheres, others like discs; many are horn or tooth-shaped. Many are, oddly enough, hollow.

Once you have seen an abalone pearl, it can never be confused with any other type of pearl. There are no clear guides for judging them, but generally the same factors used to evaluate other types of pearls apply — color, luster, orient, shape, blemishes or skin perfection, nacre thickness and size (see Chapter 5).

In terms of color, the magentas and peacock greens and blues are the most desirable and command the highest prices. Most will have a brownish or discolored area; this is typical and does not usually diminish the value to any great extent. The higher the luster and iridescence ("orient"), the rarer and more valuable the pearl. The smoothness of the surface and freedom from blemishes is also very important, but keep in mind that it is extremely rare to find an abalone pearl with a "flawless" surface or symmetrical shape; truly round or spherical abalone pearls are virtually unknown. Look for uniform nacre growth without "pockets" or "depressions" just under the surface. Very high orient or iridescence is important, and shapes that spark the imagination are also prized. As with other pearls, size can't be ignored. Most abalone pearls are the size of pebbles, but they can be quite large. An abalone weighing 471.10 carats is perhaps the world's largest, but it is brownish and the quality is poor.

The "perfect" abalone is virtually non-existent, but when one comes close to perfection, its price will be exceptionally high. An exceptionally fine, wedge-shaped abalone pearl weighing 118.57 carats was found by a Pacific coast diver several years ago; it was a very rare gem exhibiting a strong green body color, rich iridescence, and a spotless surface. It was valued at over $140,000.

Conch Pearls

The conch pearl (pronounced "konk") is in a class by itself. It is not, technically speaking, considered a true pearl by most gemologists because it is not produced by a bivalve mollusc, nor is it a "nacreous" creation (created by the build up of numerous concentric layers of nacre). Nonetheless, few would disagree that it is indeed a rare and beautiful gem, one that can command a very high price.

The conch "pearl" is produced by the giant univalve conch that is found throughout the Caribbean. The conch is in great demand for its meat (conch fritters are delicious) and for its shell, which is used to make cameos and for garden decoration. Some people even pride themselves on their ability to "blow" the conch shell, and it was used by island tribes in the past to sound an alarm when danger approached.

Conch pearls, like other pearls, are made of calcium carbonate, but they lack the build-up of layer upon layer of nacre responsible for the characteristic luster and iridescence associated with pearls. We call such pearls *non-nacreous* pearls. Most non-nacreous pearls are dull and unattractive, with little value; the conch is an exception.

The conch pearl can be strikingly beautiful and very costly. It has a distinctive porcelain-like sheen combined with a unique "flame pattern" on the surface. This flame pattern resembles delicate, wavy, whitish lines covering the entire surface of the pearl. If you've ever seen wet silk, the pattern is similar. This "flame" structure separates it immediately from nacreous pearls, and from coral, with which it might otherwise be confused.

The chance of finding a conch pearl is slim: about one for every 10,000 to 15,000 conch shells opened. Most have pleasing symmetrical shapes; on rare occasions, round conch pearls have been found. Most are beige, ivory or brown in color, but they are also found in salmon-orange, lilac, pink and deep rose shades. (The color may fade if exposed to strong sunlight for a prolonged time.) While shape and size are important, quality is judged primarily by the intensity of the color and pattern. The most prized conch pearl is nearly spherical with an intense flame pattern over a deep pink, lilac or orange-pink color. Symmetrical oval, teardrop and button shapes are also highly prized. Most conch pearls are small. The largest known conch pearl is a dark brown gem that comes from the "horse conch." It is football-shaped, weighs over 111 carats, and measures 27.47 millimeters in size.

Conch pearls are in great demand in Europe and the Middle East. The New York jewelry salon of Harry Winston created a magnificent conch pearl and diamond necklace, with accompanying conch pearl and diamond earrings, for an unidentified client, and the German jewelry firm Hemmerle has just completed a magnificent jewelry creation using the dark brown conch pearl mentioned above, the world's largest (see color insert). It is priced at $100,000.

There are other types of non-nacreous pearls which may be encountered. Most have little luster, little or no iridescence, and have little value.

Conch pearls and the giant conch shell

Pearls have become an essential for any well-dressed woman today, and increasingly for men as well, yet most buyers feel overwhelmed and intimidated by all the choices, and the widely differing prices. But with just a little knowledge, you'll be surprised by how quickly you can learn to see and understand variations in characteristics and quality.

Part Three
The Difference Quality Makes

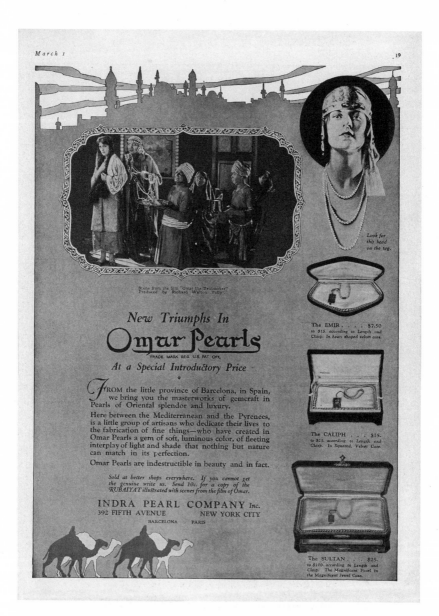

Scene from the film "Omar the Tentmaker"
Produced by Richard Walton Tully

New Triumphs In

Omar Pearls

TRADE MARK REG. U.S. PAT. OFF.

At a Special Introductory Price

FROM the little province of Barcelona, in Spain,
we bring you the masterworks of gemcraft in
Pearls of Oriental splendor and luxury.

Here between the Mediterranean and the Pyrenees,
is a little group of artisans who dedicate their lives to
the fabrication of fine things—who have created in
Omar Pearls a gem of soft, luminous color, of fleeting
interplay of light and shade that nothing but nature
can match in its perfection.

Omar Pearls are indestructible in beauty and in fact.

*Sold at better shops everywhere. If you cannot get
the genuine write us. Send 10c. for a copy of the
RUBAIYAT illustrated with scenes from the film of Omar.*

INDRA PEARL COMPANY Inc.
392 FIFTH AVENUE   NEW YORK CITY
BARCELONA   PARIS

*Look for
this head
on the tag.*

The EMIR $7.50
to $15. according to Length and
Clasp. In heart shaped velvet case.

The CALIPH . . . $15.
to $25. according to Length and
Clasp. In Squared Velvet Case.

The SULTAN . . . $25.
to $100. according to Length and
Clasp. The Magnificent Pearl in
the Magnificent Jewel Case.

1924 ad for Omar *simulated* pearls — this is very unclear from the ad. Today such ads are a
violation of U.S. Federal Trade Commission guidelines.

Chapter 5

Quality — Key to Lasting Beauty

More important than knowing what type of pearl you have is knowing whether or not you have a good pearl, and how to tell the difference. Just as there are differences in quality that affect the beauty, desirability and cost of diamonds and colored gemstones, there are differences in quality that affect the beauty, desirability, and cost of pearls.

The same factors are judged when evaluating natural and cultured pearls, but different standards are used to arrive at the overall quality classification, that is, "poor," "good," "fine," and so on. Here we will limit our discussion of quality to the evaluation of *cultured pearls*. To develop an appreciation for quality differences in natural pearls, we suggest taking advantage of any opportunity you have to see and compare natural pearls to develop your own eye for differences in each factor. This can be done by viewing natural pearls in museum collections, at auction viewings, in antique jewelry exhibitions, and so on. Your jeweler may also be able to locate natural pearls for you to see. As you compare them, keep in mind the factors described below, noting the range in variations. It won't be long before you are able to distinguish unusually fine natural pearls from those that are fair or poor quality.

Quality Is the #1 Consideration in Selecting Cultured Pearls

Understanding quality differences in cultured pearls is perhaps even more important than for diamonds and colored gems because quality differences can affect how long the beauty of pearls will *last*. A fine pearl is a gem that will stand the test of time, a thing of lasting beauty to be enjoyed and cherished from generation to generation; a poor quality pearl can quickly lose its beauty, in some cases after only months!

Finding the Perfect Balance for *Lasting* Beauty

Each pearl producer must decide how to best balance all the factors involved so that a lovely pearl is produced, at an affordable price, without unnecessary risk. It is truly a game of chance. The longer the pearl remains in the oyster, the greater the potential loss in the event of disease, natural disaster, or other calamity. In terms of quality, more time means thicker nacre and, potentially, a more lustrous, longer-lasting pearl. But the longer the pearl is in the oyster, the greater the extent to which other desirable characteristics — shape, color and surface perfection — may be adversely affected. As we have mentioned, for example, since the nucleus starts out round — and since nacre doesn't crystallize uniformly around the entire nucleus, at the same time — it may become increasingly out-of-round as nacre builds up around it, and the surface may become blemished.

Pearl producers must constantly weigh potential benefits against risks, but there is no standard guideline. Some producers take greater risks than others in an effort to produce the rarest and most beautiful pearls, allowing the pearl to remain in the oyster for the longest possible time; these are the costliest cultured pearls. Others try to minimize every risk, often by shortening the cultivation period.

Today the cultivation period among many producers has been reduced from 18 months to less than one year, with the average running at about eight months. Although improvements in nutrition and overall care have resulted in improved quality and better nacre production by the oyster, most industry experts agree this is too short a period to pqÊ-duce pearls with nacre thick enough to assure lasting beauty; thin-nacre pearls cost much less, but they have no longevity and there are questions as to whether they should be purchased at any price. Many pearls are now sold with nacre so thin they won't last any time at all; others have somewhat thicker nacre, and look better, but still won't stand the test of time. For this reason, nacre thickness may be the most important factor to consider when selecting pearls. Fortunately, this is a difference you can often see with your eye!

Differences Can Be Seen with the Eye

An unusual characteristic of pearls not found in most other

gems is that quality differences can usually be seen with one's own eye! The ability to see differences comes fairly quickly once you understand what to look for as you consider various pearls, and how to examine them; you'll be surprised how quickly you will start to notice the differences and become more selective.

We recommend first using the eye alone; this is all you usually need. In some cases, it may also be helpful to use the jeweler's loupe.

How to Use a Loupe

The loupe

To check drilled pearls more closely, or to examine surface blemishes, it also may be helpful to use a loupe (pronounced "loop"), a special type of magnifier used by jewelers. It should be a 10-power, *triplet* type — a triplet has been corrected for distortion and color fringing — in a black housing (not chrome or gold-plated).

With a few minutes' practice you can easily learn to use the loupe to examine pearls. Here's how:

1. Hold the loupe between the thumb and forefinger of one hand.

2. Hold the pearl or strand similarly in the other hand.

3. Bring both hands together so that the fleshy parts just below the thumbs are pushed together and braced by the lower portion of each hand just above the wrists.

4. Align the loupe with what you are examining so that the item is about one inch away from the loupe.

5. Now move the hands/loupe/ pearl — keeping them all braced together — up to your nose or cheek, bringing the loupe as close to the eye as possible; if you wear eyeglasses, you do not have to remove them.

Using the loupe

6. Get a steady hand. It's important to have steady hands for careful examination. With your hands still together and braced against some part of your face, put your elbows on a table or countertop. (If a table isn't available, brace your arms against your chest or rib cage). If you do this properly, you will have a steady hand.

Practice with the loupe, keeping it approximately one inch (more or less) from the eye, and about an inch from the pearl. Learn to see through it clearly. It is difficult to focus initially, but with a little practice it will become easy. You can practice focusing on any object that is difficult to see — the pores in your skin or a strand of hair.

Play with the item being examined. Rotate it slowly, tilt it back and forth while rotating it, look at it from different angles and different directions. It won't take long before you are able to focus easily on anything you wish to examine. If you aren't sure about your technique, a knowledgeable jeweler will be happy to help you learn to use the loupe correctly.

What You Will See with the Loupe

With practice and experience, a loupe can tell even the amateur a great deal. You won't be able to see what a trained gemologist will see, but here are some ways it can be helpful for the beginner when examining pearls:
1. *To check the drill hole* to better estimate the size of the hole; to check for line of demarcation between nucleus and nacre (indicating *cultured* rather than natural); and to spot traces of dye (traces of dye may be seen just inside the drill hole).
2. *To examine surface blemishes more carefully*, to spot cracks and missing nacre that would indicate poor nacre quality or nacre that is too thin.
3. *To see surface characteristics that might indicate imitation* since the surface of cultured (and natural) pearls looks very different from imitations; once you've observed the surface of a pearl you know is cultured, and compare it with one you know to be imitation, it's easy to spot imitations.

How to Examine Pearls to See Quality Differences

Before beginning, it is very important to understand there is no internationally accepted grading system for pearls. Pearl dealers and jewelry retailers use their own systems. These systems often use the same alphabetical nomenclature — we often see pearls graded "Triple A" (AAA), "Double A" (AA), "A" "B," or "C" — but since they aren't based on the same standards or criteria, they don't necessarily reflect comparable qualities. With no standardized criteria, the quality represented by one seller may be much higher, or lower, than that of another; one jeweler's "Triple A" quality pearl may be the equivalent of another's "C" grade.

You cannot assume that you are comparing comparable pearls based on terms such as "AAA," "AA" and so on. With pearls, you must learn how — and what — to examine.

- **View pearls against a neutral background.** When examining pearls, view them against a neutral, non-glossy background. A very light gray is ideal, or a flat white background (such as white tissue paper, always available in jewelry stores). *Never view pearls against only a black background* — pearls look very beautiful worn against black, but black makes it difficult to see subtle, costly differences.

- **View pearls in cool-white fluorescent or daylight light.** Avoid intense spotlights or incandescent light (luster will always appear more intense under strong direct light such as sunlight or spotlights; it will always look lower in diffused light, as on a cloudy day, or under fluorescent lights). Keep in mind that the type of light in which you examine pearls will affect what you see, so *pearls being considered should be viewed and compared in the same light.* When possible, compare them in the same place, at the same time of day. (Pearls can look different from one geographic location to another for the same reason — differences in light from hemisphere to hemisphere).

- **View pearls at a right angle to your body.** When comparing strands of pearls, as in necklaces or bracelets, lay them on the neutral background at a right angle to your body so that the strands are close to one another but not touching. This will make it easier to see differences, especially in color and luster.

The Six Factors That Affect Pearl Quality and Value

Now that you know *how* to view pearls to make quality comparisons, let's talk about *what* to examine. Regardless of the type of pearl, or whether it is natural or cultured, the following factors must be evaluated to determine whether or not it is a fine pearl that will give you lasting beauty:

- Luster & Orient
- Nacre Thickness and Quality
- Color

- Surface Perfection
- Shape
- Size

Nacre thickness, and the quality of the nacre, have a greater effect on the beauty of a pearl than any other factor — and with a cultured pearl, on how long it will last. For this reason, I consider it the most important factor. However, we will discuss "luster" and "orient" first because this is what we notice first — what makes the pearl special — and because *differences in luster and orient provide visual clues to nacre thickness.*

The combination of the lovely reflective glow we call luster and the soft iridescent play-of-color we call *orient* is what distinguishes the pearl from all other gems. They are also the most easily seen indicators of a pearl's quality, and of its potential for lasting beauty.

Luster

When you see a fine pearl, the first thing you notice is its lustrous glow. Luster is not a superficial "shine" such as you see in imitation pearls, but an intense brightness that results from rays of light travelling through the numerous layers of nacre and being reflected back from *within* the pearl. One might describe it as a "shine with *depth.*" In a pearl with good luster, there will be a sharp contrast between the pearl's brightest area (the part in direct light) and the shaded area; sometimes the contrast creates the illusion of a "ball" within the pearl — the more intense the image of the ball, the better the luster. Luster is evaluated on the sharpness or brightness of the reflection, which depends upon the quality and the quantity of light reflected from its surface. This, in turn, depends upon the quality and thickness of the nacre produced by the mollusc. The thicker the nacre (and the smaller and more transparent the microscopic crystals comprising it), the better the luster. When numerous layers of nacre have crystallized properly and each layer is well aligned with the other, the result is an exquisite, intensely lustrous pearl.

How to Judge Luster

Anyone buying pearls should take time to learn to evaluate luster and, in particular, to recognize what is acceptable and what is not acceptable; in particular, when luster is too *low.* Low luster not only reduces the beauty of the pearl, but can provide an indicator of very thin nacre. With Japanese pearls, low "chalky" luster usually indicates a *very* thin nacre coating that can quickly crack, peel, or simply wear off, leaving just mother-of-pearl beads. (Imitation pearls will give longer pleasure than poor quality, chalky cultured pearls, and usually at a lower cost!).

Rule #1: *Look for pearls with high luster.* Luster is judged from *very high* to *very low.* A pearl with very high luster will seem vibrant, and the light reflection (the intensity of the "ball") will be sharp and bright; a pearl with very low luster is dull, and the reflection hazy, chalky or non-existent. To judge luster —

- **Roll the pearls to view them from all sides** to make sure the luster is uniform.

- **Examine them under a light source such as a fluorescent lamp,** looking for reflections of the light off the surface, paying particular attention to the brightness or sharpness of the reflections. Avoid strong, direct light. If the available light is too strong, hold your hand over the pearls to shade them, and examine in the shadowed area.

Top quality Japanese Akoya cultured pearls can have a higher luster than other white round cultured pearls because of the water temperature in which they are produced. Cold water causes slower nacre production, which normally results in superior crystallization and overall nacre quality. When the nacre quality is good, and it is exceptionally thick, Japanese Akoya pearls can have incredible lustrousness. The luster can also be very chalky, indicating very thin nacre, or poor quality nacre.

Iridescent Orient

When the nacre is well formed, and very thick, you will observe *orient,* a soft, iridescent play-of-color across the pearl's surface. This iridescent quality is only present when the layers of nacre are thick enough to cause a prismatic effect (white light divided into all the colors of the rainbow) as the light travels through them.

Round cultured pearls that exhibit this iridescent orient are highly prized and sought by connoisseurs. Today it is rare to find round cultured pearls that possess this sublime characteristic, but it can frequently be seen in the irregular shapes of baroque pearls, adding to their allure. For orient to be present, each layer of nacre must be well crystallized and aligned, and, most important, the nacre must be *unusually thick.* This is why orient is often seen in fine natural pearls — which are all nacre — and in fine, older strands of Japanese cultured pearls, which have thicker nacre than those normally being produced today. An iridescent orient can also be seen in the irregular shapes of baroque pearls, where the shape causes depressions in which the nacre collects in deep "pools", and in pearls with very long cultivation periods, such as South Sea pearls, American freshwater cultured pearls, and fine quality, all-nacre Chinese "potato" pearls.

Luster and orient are important not only because they affect the pearl's beauty, but as we continue to stress, because they are a visible indicator of nacre thickness and quality.

Nacre Thickness and Quality

Whether natural or cultured, the *thickness* of the pearl's nacre and its *quality* is what gives the pearl its unique beauty. The thicker the nacre and the better the nacre quality, the more lustrous and iridescent — the more exquisite — the pearl.

Nacre thickness determines the pearl's longevity — the thicker the nacre, the longer the life of the pearl; the thinner the nacre, the shorter its life. Finding the right balance to get an adequate nacre thickness without jeopardizing other factors such as shape and surface perfection takes skill and experience, as mentioned earlier. The farmers producing the finest, most beautiful cultured pearls are those who allow the nucleus to remain in the oyster the longest possible time between the implanting and harvesting, to obtain the thickest possible nacre coating.

Nacre quality determines how the light travels through the layers. Sometimes pearls with thick nacre fail to exhibit the intensity of luster or orient that is expected. This normally results from the particular way in which the layers of nacre crystallized. For reasons we don't fully understand, the nacre crystals have not formed with a good transparency, the layers are not uniform, or they are not properly aligned. We do know that the *rate* at which nacre is produced affects its quality. If nacre is produced *too fast*, it will be less transparent. The result is a pearl with lower luster; light enters the pearl, but less is reflected back. This is not necessarily bad. One must always weigh the importance of one factor against another. A thick-nacre South Sea pearl with subdued luster will be more affordable than one with higher luster; it can still have a lovely character and, costing less, might enable you to acquire a larger size.

There seems to be a connection between nacre quality, water temperature and stability of overall water conditions. Pearl-producing oysters in the warmer waters of Australia, Tahiti, the Cook Islands, Philippines, and Indonesia produce nacre *much* faster than the Japanese or Chinese; some experts estimate production to be *fifteen to twenty times* faster. This means that even if the pearl is left in the oyster for the same amount of time as Japanese pearls — and fine South Sea pearls usually have a *longer* cultivation period — the nacre would be much thicker. Fine South Sea cultured pearls often exhibit an iridescent orient because of their thicker nacre. As we have said, this is rare today in white

Japanese pearls, but fine Japanese pearls usually exhibit a much brighter, sharper luster attributed to the colder waters. Japanese pearls that exhibit *both* the intense lustrousness for which they are known *and* a soft, iridescent orient indicating thick nacre are very rare. Such pearls, however, are among the most beautiful and prized of all.

To have a lustrous, iridescent pearl, the nacre quality must be good and the nacre layers must be thick; it is a combination of the two that affects the quantity and quality of light reflected back from the surface. While there may be pearls with thick nacre that don't exhibit rich luster and orient because of how the layers crystallized, **there are no pearls with rich luster and orient that do not have fine, *thick* nacre.** Any pearl that exhibits a rich lustrousness is one that has thick nacre; and, since nacre must be thick to produce the iridescent effect we call orient, any pearl which shows this lovely iridescence must have thick nacre.

How to Judge Nacre Thickness

In natural pearls, the pearl is entirely nacre; in saltwater cultured pearls, it can range from very thin to very thick, averaging about 10%-15% of the total pearl diameter, and rarely exceeding 30%. Nacre thickness of South Sea cultured pearls is much greater than any others and the finest may be 40%-50% nacre.

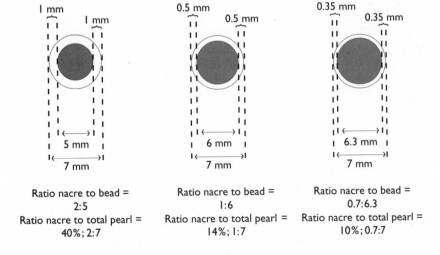

Ratio nacre to bead =
2:5
Ratio nacre to total pearl =
40%; 2:7

Ratio nacre to bead =
1:6
Ratio nacre to total pearl =
14%; 1:7

Ratio nacre to bead =
0.7:6.3
Ratio nacre to total pearl =
10%; 0.7:7

When nacre is too thin, pearls will not last. With pearls commanding the prices they do, we don't think anyone would *knowingly* buy pearls that won't last. So here are some ways to estimate nacre thickness, and avoid pearls with thin nacre:

- **Look for orient.** If the pearl has a uniform iridescence playing across its surface, it has very thick nacre. Don't worry about any pearl that displays a lovely orient.

- **Note the intensity of luster.** Pearls with a bright, intense luster that sharply reflects nearby images, will have a good nacre thickness; pearls that look very dull or chalky probably have very thin nacre or poor quality nacre.

- **Check for cracks and peeling.** Pearls with very thin nacre crack easily, often revealing the nucleus. Also, thin nacre will peel or wear off over time. In some cases, the nacre is so thin that new pearls have already begun to peel, leaving small areas of exposed mother-of-pearl. Check carefully for any exposed mother-of-pearl.

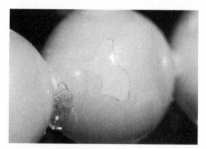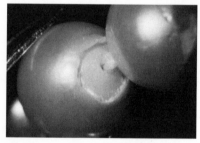

Left: Pearl with *very* thin nacre. Notice peeling in center and near drill hole.
Right: Notice nacre broken away from drill hole.

- **View the pearl near the drill hole with a loupe.** Use the technique described on page 61. Shine a very bright light, the brighter the better, a few inches over the hole. Examine the hole, noting where the nacre ends and the mother-of-pearl bead begins; the nacre is always lighter. Mentally estimate thickness.

- **Check for banding.** When viewing pearls with a strong light as described above, check to see whether you can see any alternating lighter and darker areas or bands; if so, you are seeing the "layers" of the mother-of-pearl nucleus, and this indicates a thinner nacre than is ideal.

Cross section of good Akoya pearl, showing thick nacre.

> ### Grading Nacre Thickness in Japanese Pearl Strands
>
> • **Very thick** — At least 0.5 mm on all pearls
>
> • **Thick** — At least 0.5 mm on most pearls
>
> • **Medium** — Between 0.35 mm and 0.5 mm on most pearls
>
> • **Thin** — Between 0.25 mm and 0.35 mm on most pearls
>
> • **Very Thin** — 0.25 mm or less on most pearls

In cases where you can't be sure of nacre thickness, we *strongly recommend submitting pearls to a gem testing laboratory for a report indicating nacre thickness.* Only a few labs now provide this information, but more and more are beginning to do so, if requested. (See List of Laboratories in Chapter 17.)

Color: Silvery White to Blackest Night, and a Rainbow in Between

Color is an important factor to consider for several reasons. Individuals have very personal preferences in terms of color based on their own skin, eye, and hair color and should select a color that is best suited to themselves. Color also affects cost because some are rarer than others. Perhaps most important, there are more colors of cultured pearls being produced today than ever before, offering unusual and distinctive alternatives to traditional white pearls, and additional pearl choices for any occasion.

How to Evaluate Color

For white cultured pearls, there are two principal elements involved in evaluating color: *body color* and *overtone*. Some also include "orient" in the evaluation of color, and when it is present, it certainly affects the overall impression of the color seen. The "body color" refers to the basic color, i.e., white, cream, yellow. The "overtone" refers to the presence of a secondary color (its "tint"), usually a pinkish, greenish, silver or blue tint. When we speak of color in pearls, we are referring to the *combination* of the body color and overtone. White-rosé would mean white pearls with a rose-colored overtone (tint); naturally white pearls with a blush of pink are rare and expensive. Creamier pearls are less rare and more affordable. In white pearls, the rarest and costliest overtone is "pink" (rosé); a green overtone is considered less desirable in white pearls, and its presence reduces value.

In pearls that have a "fancy color" or hue — a distinctive color clearly distinct from the "white"/ "off-white" category — there is an additional color element: tone. This refers to color *intensity*, and is graded from "Light" to "Dark." A dark yellow pearl, for example, will have a much richer color than a light yellow pearl; it is also much rarer, more desirable, and costlier.

In naturally "black" cultured pearls, the color can range from light gray to dark gray to black, and also includes blue and green; overtones are usually green or pink (rosé). In black pearls, a green overtone is the rarest and most costly, especially when it results in an intense "peacock" color. A pink overtone in gray or black pearls creates mauve or "eggplant" colors. These are less rare and costly, but still lovely and distinctive.

Cultured pearls are available in many colors — white, gray, black, pink, green, blue, gold — from many parts of the world. The Philippines are known for yellow and golden pearls; Tahiti, other islands of French Polynesia, and the Cook Islands for naturally black cultured pearls (see Chapter 8). Untreated, natural color Chinese round freshwater cultured strands consisting of many colors all strung together, called *harlequin* pearls, are also highly sought.

Fancy-color pearls can be very rare and, depending upon the color that interests you, difficult to find. Anyone searching for a fancy-color should take time to visit several very fine jewelers to see the full range of colors available. This will help you select a color with which you will always be pleased.

Techniques to Artificially Enhance Color

While pearls occur in a range of colors naturally, sometimes the colors are induced by artificial techniques. Today most white Japanese cultured pearls have been bleached to make them whiter, then *dyed* to impart tints. White pearls that have been dyed after being drilled for jewelry use (as in a necklace) can usually be detected easily by a qualified gemologist. By examining with a loupe at the drill hole, you may even be able to detect the color enhancement yourself. If the pearl is dyed, and if you can see the line of demarcation between the nucleus and the nacre, there will be a visible concentration of pink or reddish dye in the conchiolin layer (which is spongy and absorbs the dye).

For unusual colors, especially the costly black variety, we recommend sending pearls to a gem-testing lab with sophisticated equipment to know for sure whether or not the color is natural.

There are no standard systems for describing or communicating color, so once again it is up to you to look at pearls carefully, developing your own eye to see differences in the body color, overtone and tone.

Surface Perfection

Think of the pearl's surface as you would your own skin. Just as our own is rarely completely free of little imperfections, so it is with the pearl. Surface perfection refers to the pearl's "skin" being free of such things as small blisters, pimples, spots, or cracks. Imperfections may also appear as dark spots, small indentations, welts or blisters, or surface bumps. While occasional small blemishes are not uncommon, if large or numerous they are unsightly. A pearl with sizable or numerous blemishes may also be less durable. The cleaner the skin, the rarer and costlier. If drilled, the closer the blemish to the drill hole, the less it detracts from both appearance and value.

Right pearl has smooth surface while left pearl shows pronounced blemish.

Sometimes dark spots result from contact with perfumes, oils, cosmetics, and so on. If superficial, they can sometimes be removed by rubbing a mild polishing compound gently across the surface with a chamois cloth.

How to Judge Surface Perfection

- **Examine in several types of light.** While diffused light is normally best for comparing quality factors in pearls, when checking for blemishes, an intense light may highlight certain types. When examining pearls for blemishes, it may be helpful to check them with both diffused light and an intense bright light.

- **Examine against a dark background.** A light background is normally best for comparing most pearl characteristics, but when checking for blemishes, it is sometimes easier to spot them against a dark background.

- **Examine while rolling.** Place the pearl or pearl strand on a flat surface and roll it to be sure you have examined all sides, and so that the light catches any blemish and highlights it.

- **Hold the pearls up** and examine them while holding them out in front of you, at eye level.

Practically speaking, there is no such thing as a "flawless" pearl; they are exceptionally rare. In strands, this is even truer. You must decide what is important to you in terms of color, shape, size, and so on, and then balance the factors accordingly. I recommend sacrificing the surface perfection somewhat rather than other factors. Selecting pearls that are slightly blemished may enable you to purchase pearls with thicker nacre, a more desirable color, or larger size. Also keep in mind that *if the pearl has intense luster*, most blemishes won't even be noticed; high luster helps conceal them! A dull chalky white pearl, however, will show every blemish, no matter how small.

Avoid pearls with cracks. Cracks can be serious and may lead to peeling nacre, especially if the nacre is thin.

Shape

Shape in pearls is divided into three categories: spherical, symmetrical, and baroque. The rarest and most valuable is the spherical or round pearl; these are judged on their degree of "sphericity" or roundness. While *fine* pearls that are perfectly round are extremely rare, the closer a pearl comes to being perfectly round, the more expensive it will be. Pearls with shapes such as the teardrop or pear-shape are symmetrical pearls, and are judged on proportioning, outline, and good symmetry; that is, whether they have a nice, pleasing, well-balanced shape. Symmetrical pearls are usually less expensive than round pearls — although there are some exceptions — but much more expensive than baroque pearls, which are irregularly shaped pearls.

Any strand of pearls should be well matched for shape, and when worn give the appearance of uniformity.

New shapes are being produced today that don't really fall into any of the three categories above. These include *"coin"* pearls, which look like flat coins; thin, rectangular *"bars"*; *"potato"* pearls, which resemble an oval potato; and *"ringed"* or *"circlé"* pearls, which exhibit concentric rings from top to bottom.

Terms such as semi-round and semi-baroque are also used. These are terms applied to pearls that are "out of round" but not so much that the irregular shape is interesting, or distinctive. These cost much less than other shapes.

Black "circlé" or "ring" pearl beside a black pear shape pearl.

Round, off-round, and asymmetrical baroque pearls. Bottom: Oval or acorn shape; teardrop or pear shape; button, twin, and hourglass symmetrical baroque pearls.

Differences in shape affect value. The top strand is "round" and is priced higher than each of the strands beneath, which show progressively greater deviations from "round."

White "acorn" shape cultured pearl earrings

Size

Natural pearls are sold by *weight*. Until relatively recently, they were weighed in "grains," with four grains equal to one carat. Today, however, they are usually sold by carat weight. Cultured pearls are sold by *millimeter size* (one millimeter equals approximately ¹⁄₂₅ inch): their measurement indicates the *diameter* of round pearls, and the *length and width* if not round. The larger the pearl, the greater the cost. A 2 millimeter cultured pearl is considered very small, whereas Akoya cultured pearls over 8 millimeters are considered very large; in South Sea pearls, an 8 millimeter pearl is small, 13-15 millimeters is average, and over 16 millimeters is very large.

Large cultured pearls are rarer, and more expensive. In Akoya pearls there is a dramatic jump in the cost after 7 ½ millimeters. The price jumps upward rapidly with each half-millimeter from 8 millimeters up. In South Sea and Tahitian pearls, cost is also dramatically affected as sizes exceed 15 millimeters.

As we have mentioned, even though size is determined primarily by the size of the nucleus implanted in the mollusc, the larger the implant the greater the rejection and death rate. In addition, the larger the nucleus, the more blemished, discolored, and misshapen the pearls become, reducing the number of fine pearls even further. This is why they are so much more expensive than smaller pearls.

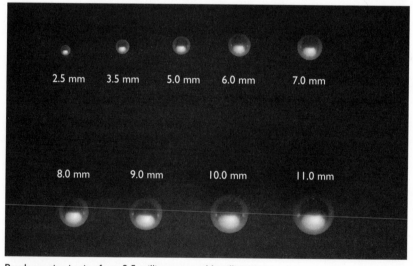

Pearls ranging in size from 2.5 millimeters to 11 millimeters.

The "Make" Can Also "Make" a Difference

Another factor affecting the value of any pearl item which has been strung, as in a necklace, is the precision which went into the matching of the pearls; this is called the "make." Consider how well matched the strand is in size, shape, color, luster, and surface texture. Graduated pearls also require careful sizing. Failure to match carefully will detract from both appearance of the item and its value.

It is also very important to check that the pearls are all *center* drilled; off-center drilling will result in pearls that will never lay properly. Off-center drilling will greatly reduce value.

Chapter 6

Artificial Enhancements Used on Lackluster Pearls

With all things beautiful, rare, and costly, humankind tries to improve, imitate, and duplicate. It has been this way since time began. Today virtually all colored gemstones are imitated, duplicated, and "improved," and cultured pearls have not been ignored. As with other gems, some of the methods used are considered "acceptable" while others are not. It is important to be aware of the types of treatments being used, what is acceptable and what is not, and how they affect the final pearl product in terms of appearance, cost and, most of all, durability.

All pearls are processed after removal from the mollusc. Routine processing will not harm them, and usually involves little more than washing to remove odors and residues from the pores of the pearl's surface. This can be accomplished with mild sudsy warm water and a mild abrasive such as salt. The pearls are put into "tumbling" drums with the solution, and tumbled together for a brief time.

Routine tumbling is performed by all cultured pearl producers, and is perfectly safe.

Excessive Processing and Treatment Can Harm Pearls

Certain types of cultured pearls are routinely subjected to *extensive* processing and various other treatments that may have an adverse effect on durability, and thus to the life of the pearl. These include extensive tumbling, often with wax or polishing compounds, buffing with polishing compounds, coating pearl surfaces, chemical bleaching and dyeing. Here are some practices to be aware of and to guard against:

Enhancement of Luster and Surface Perfection

Since lustrousness is so desirable in a pearl, and because it is usually very low in poor quality pearls, some producers employ artificial methods along with routine processing to create an *impression* of lustrousness. The following enhancements result in a temporary surface shine only.

- **Extensive tumbling** is used by some producers to remove unsightly surface blemishes and dark spots, and to improve the shape of the pearl. Nacre is durable because of its very compact structure, but it is not very *hard*. Depending upon the tumbling process used, some of the nacre may actually be wearing off as the pearl is being tumbled — the longer the tumbling, the greater the amount of nacre removed.

- **Buffing** is used by some producers to remove blemishes, improve the shape, and to add a surface shine. Here the pearls are "buffed" against a rapidly moving abrasive wheel with a very mild abrasive compound. It is very effective, but removes more nacre than simple tumbling. *Beeswax and other polishing compounds* are sometimes used while tumbling or buffing — beeswax is soft and won't remove the nacre; harder compounds will remove nacre.

- **Tumbling with beeswax** is done primarily to improve the pearl's lustrousness. Wax is melted in very hot pans and then bamboo chips are added. After the chips have become saturated with beeswax, they are placed together with the pearls in tumbling drums. As they tumble around together in the drum, a waxy coating is acquired by the pearls. Since the bamboo chips are softer than pearl, the pearls aren't scratched or nacre thickness eroded. This wax coating imparts a lustrousness, but it is temporary and will wear off in a short period of time — and if you clean your pearls in an ultrasonic cleaner, even faster!

- **Extensive buffing with chemical polishing compounds** is sometimes done to remove more unsightly surface imperfections and to increase surface shine. Chemical compounds create a longer-lasting shine than wax, but it is still *temporary* and, even worse, these compounds often remove layers of nacre, reducing the life of the pearl.

- **Coating** with lacquer or "pearlessence" — an epoxy and ground fish-scale concoction used to create imitation pearls — to create a surface shine. Lacquer wears off quickly; pearlessence may last longer.

In the case of poor quality *mabé* pearls, pearlessence and dye are often applied to the *inside* of the pearl, just beneath the nacre (since mabé pearls are actually *hollow* blisters that are cut from the shell and then filled with another substance to increase durability, it is easy to coat the inside with pearlessence *prior to filling it*).

This practice is not accepted as a fair trade practice and is considered fraudulent; nonetheless, it occurs. While there are some higher quality mabé pearls with thick nacre, especially South Sea mabés, one must be on guard against mabés treated in this way because their thin nacre will peel and crack very easily. *When buying mabé pearls, pay particular attention to lustrousness.* However, you may not be able to recognize a pearl treated in this way. Should your mabé pearl begin to peel, or if it cracks prematurely despite proper care, we suggest you return it to your jeweler.

Any treatment that reduces nacre thickness is detrimental to the life of the pearl. Pearls that are buffed or tumbled extensively lose some of their nacre and are at greater risk of cracking and chipping. If nacre was thin prior to treatment, the result may be pearls with nacre that will more quickly wear off, leaving only mother-of-pearl beads.

Be especially careful not to mistake shallow shine for the rich luster that indicates a deep, thick nacre. If in doubt, ask that the pearls be submitted to a laboratory for a report on nacre thickness (see List of Laboratories in Chapter 17 for laboratories that provide this information).

Techniques to Alter Color

Whitening the color of pearls has taken place for centuries. In the case of natural pearls, however, it was a natural process whereby pearls were sun-bleached on rugs for a period of time. The rugs could be easily rotated to expose various parts of the pearl so color would be uniform. Many pearls today are also whitened, but normally the whitening process involves chemical bleaching. In addition to whitening, color is further enhanced by dyeing or other artificial techniques. Bleaching and dyeing is done to create continuity of color, which people have come to expect in cultured pearls as a result of advertising and promotion.

Here again, most South Sea pearls, naturally black pearls from Tahiti and other parts of the South Pacific, and American freshwater cultured pearls are the only pearls being cultured today that are not normally subjected to chemical bleaching and dyeing as part of routine processing.

• **Chemical bleaching** is done to make pearls whiter. This is now a common practice among many producers.

This process is especially detrimental to thin-nacre pearls

because chemical bleaching reduces the hardness of the nacre, making the pearl softer and more susceptible to deterioration from normal wear. If the pearl has a good nacre thickness, this probably won't seriously affect its durability; if the pearl has thin nacre, chemical bleaching will further weaken it.

All pearls with *thin* nacre *must* be bleached because the nacre is so thin that the brownish conchiolin shows through, creating an undesirable dark color; in thick nacre pearls, the dark conchiolin won't show through so bleaching may not be necessary. (Remember that the oyster first produces a brownish layer of a substance we call "conchiolin" before producing the layers of white nacre that build up to give us the pearl.) To bleach pearls, they are first drilled and then submerged in a bleaching solution which takes the brownish color out of the conchiolin layer, thus whitening the pearl. Bleaching also produces a more uniform surface whiteness.

• **Dyeing** to create a more desirable color is an increasingly common practice and goes hand-in-hand with bleaching.

The bleaching often results in a pearl that is too white, making it seem lifeless. The pearls are then soaked in a dye solution, usually pink, to give them a softer, warmer look that enhances desirability. Naturally white pearls with a lovely pink or "rosé" blush are very rare and highly prized; most of today's pink-white (rosé-white) pearls have obtained their pink color artificially through the dyeing process. It is usually easy to detect using the loupe (see Chapter 5).

Pearls can also be dyed other colors. *Most black pearls under 8 millimeters in diameter have been dyed black;* most naturally black pearls are produced by a large variety of oyster in the South Pacific and start at about 8 millimeters in size. Many dyed black pearls have a different look from the natural, a look that suggests the use of dye — a "flat," very uniform black coloration that lacks any iridescence or the subtle shading and variation typical of naturally black pearls. Poor quality white pearls are used to create these dyed black pearls. They should cost a fraction of what naturally black pearls cost, and much less than good white pearls.

• **Dyeing the nucleus** to create "black" pearls is done on Akoya-type cultured pearls.

While Japan is producing *natural* black cultured pearls, many gray to black cultured pearls under 9 millimeters in diameter contain a *dyed nucleus* — dyed with an organic dye — that is responsible for the color seen on the surface. This cannot be detected without sophisticated lab tests.

• **Irradiation techniques** have been used to artificially transform inexpensive, usually off-color South Sea pearls into "black" pearls to imitate the rare and costly naturally black cultured pearls of the South Pacific.

While not commonplace, such pearls do appear in the market, so we recommend that you submit any large black pearl represented to have natural color to a laboratory for verification.

A rich *blue* mabé pearl has recently entered the marketplace. An especially beautiful color, it is being sold as both natural and irradiated. In fact, it is neither; the blue comes from using a deep blue dome-shaped plastic insert. (See the section on mabé pearls in Chapter 4.) These mabés are cut from the shell, and the very thin nacre cap is removed, and dipped in an artificial "pearlized" coating to create the illusion of an iridescent lustrousness. The deep blue plastic dome is then reinserted, filled with epoxy, and glued to a mother-of-pearl backing.

- **Silver nitrate solution** is used in China, and to a lesser extent in other countries, to transform inexpensive, off-color pearls into pearls that resemble the rare and costly natural black cultured pearls of the South Pacific.

Use of silver nitrate solution is the most damaging of all treatments used on pearls, much more damaging to the pearl than chemical bleaching, *making the nacre much softer and less durable.* It reduces the pearl's very resilience. Never buy pearls that have been treated with silver nitrate. Again, we recommend that you submit any black pearl represented to have natural color to a laboratory for verification.

There is nothing wrong with buying or selling color-enhanced pearls as long as they are properly represented and appropriately priced. Such pearls should sell for *much less* than natural-color cultured pearls.

Fine Pearls — Beauty That Needs No Artificial Enhancement

Overly short cultivation periods, excessive processing, and fraudulent treatment practices have been a source of intensifying debate and concern over the past ten years. International pearl summits have focused heavily on these issues. As a result, an increasing number of producers have begun to implement more rigid standards in the cultivation and processing of pearls, with Japan and Australia leading the way. The focus of the world's leading producers is shifting from quantity to quality; the focus now seems to be on finding more effective ways to reduce risk, but to do so without reducing the quality, beauty, and longevity of the pearl itself.

The future looks bright, but for the present you must remain attentive to quality differences. Insist on pearls with a rich, lustrous quality that assures you of thick nacre and, most of all, long lasting beauty and pleasure.

Pearl treatments and processing are meant to improve upon nature. With fine pearls, however, such efforts rarely improve them, and often diminish them. Fortunately, pearl producers are beginning to recognize this, and knowledgeable pearl connoisseurs are developing a greater appreciation for, and acceptance of, the little imperfections and differences that go hand-in-hand with any product created by nature. The lustrousness and soft iridescence of fine pearls — cultured or natural — has an allure of its own, a beauty that transcends minor "surface" imperfections!

Types of Misrepresentation

Fine pearls, natural and cultured, are very costly. The finer and rarer, the more costly. As price and demand increase, however, so do incidents of fraud and misrepresentation. For this reason, we cannot stress too strongly the importance of buying from reputable, knowledgeable jewelers. Be wary of bargains and special "promotions" which may signal inferior quality pearls that will crack, peel, and lose their beauty very quickly. Here are some practices to be aware of, and to guard against:

Selling as "natural color" pearls that have been dyed, irradiated, or treated with silver nitrate solution. As we already discussed, the color of pearls can be artificially enhanced or changed in a variety of ways. For this reason, when buying fine "natural color" pearls we recommend obtaining a laboratory report verifying that the color is natural (see List of Laboratories in Chapter 17).

Selling lacquer-coated pearls without disclosure. We have already mentioned that some pearls are coated with lacquer to improve surface lustrousness. Failure to disclose the fact that they are coated is unethical.

Misrepresenting as "round" pearls, pearls that are not. Since shape is an important factor in valuing pearls, and round pearls are rarer and more costly than those that are not round, creating the illusion of "round" is sometimes done through clever setting or stringing. A lacquer-coated filler can also be used to "round out" depressions in single, larger pearls.

Misrepresenting three-quarter pearls as full round pearls. This is done because three-quarter pearls (see Chapter 4) are significantly less expensive than round pearls. The flatter side is concealed in the setting, often a large "cup" type mounting. The cup holds the pearl in such a way that the back of the pearl cannot be seen and the flat side is concealed; the cup itself completes the illusion of roundness. Mountings used to set fine round pearls normally use cups small enough to permit you to see the full symmetry of the pearl.

Be especially careful when buying fine, round South Sea pearls because the difference in cost is dramatic. Many three-quarter South Sea pearls are being produced in the Philippines, and sold as fine round South Sea pearls, at greatly inflated prices. These may seem like "a good buy" to the unsuspecting. There is nothing wrong with buying three-quarter pearls — they can create a large, important look — as long as you know what you are buying and pay a fair price for it.

Misrepresenting half-pearls as round pearls. Half pearls, or hemisphere pearls, have a flat side where half of the pearl has been cut away to remove an unsightly blemish or defect. Natural half-pearls were very popular for use in antique jewelry, especially in pieces requiring numerous small pearls, and are sometimes mistakenly identified as round natural pearls. Examining the pearls with a loupe (see Chapter 5) will usually reveal the flat back.

Filling surface pits. This is sometimes done to conceal a particularly unsightly "pit" or hole in the pearl's surface. The pit is filled with epoxy; the epoxy is then covered with tinted lacquer or pearlessence. "Secondhand" pearls that were damaged are sometimes repaired in this manner.

Misrepresenting imitation *pearls as cultured or natural.* This may be accidental or deliberate. Many people erroneously assume that pearls that have been passed down through many generations, or been in the possession of wealthy people, must be "real." Unfortunately this is not the case; imitation pearls have been made for hundreds of years and *anyone,* including royalty, can own imitation pearls. It is usually a very easy thing to tell the real from the fake with the simple tooth test (see Chapter 3).

Misrepresenting cultured *pearls as "real" or "natural" pearls.* If buying pearls that are represented to be natural, be sure they are accompanied by a laboratory report verifying this to be true (x-ray examination is required).

Misrepresenting mollusc "hinges" as "natural" pearls. Some "natural" pearls are nothing more than the nacre coated "hinge" of a mollusc *shell* that has been cut and polished. When buying natural pearls, be sure they are accompanied by a laboratory report.

Use of misleading names is a worldwide problem. ALL OF THE FOLLOWING ARE IMITATION PEARLS:

Misnomers and What They Really Are

Misnomer	What They Really Are
Atlas pearls	Imitation; satinspar type gypsum beads
Cave pearls	Imitation; water-polished objects of calcium carbonate found in limestone caves
Kultured pearls	Imitation
Laguna pearls	Imitation
La Tausca pearls	Imitation
Majorica (Mallorca) pearls	Imitation
Nautilus pearls and Nautilus mabé pearls	Cut and polished shell from the chamber of the nautilus mollusc
Red Sea pearls	Coral beads
River strands	Imitation pearls with mother-of-pearl core
Shell mabé	Cut and polished shell from the chamber of the nautilus mollusc
South ocean pearls	Imitation pearls with mother-of-pearl core
Semi-cultured pearls	Imitation; made from cultured pearls with very poor nacre coating, over which pearlessence has been added

Part Four
Selecting Pearls to Treasure

Chapter 7

How to Choose Fine Pearls

Pearls are available today to meet every occasion, every personal style, and every budget; some are rarer than others, some much costlier than others. You may wonder how you will ever be able to balance quality, beauty and value, but it will come more easily than you can imagine, especially if you follow some simple guidelines.

First you must take time to visit fine jewelers to explore the many varieties available and decide what type of pearl you really want. **Be sure to select reputable, knowledgeable jewelers who will be able to show you a wide selection and help you learn to see subtle differences.**

Once you know what type of pearl you want, and the range in price, you must decide how to best meet your own needs.

The Secret to Getting What You Really Want

If you are like most people, you will find that you have a minimum size with which you are comfortable, and you may prefer a particular color or shape. Here are some guidelines to help you get what you want without sacrificing important quality factors.

Never sacrifice lustrousness for this is what sets the pearl apart from all other gems and gives it "life." Most of all, lustrous pearls will give you many years of pleasure and enjoyment. Such pearls are difficult to find — you won't find them just anywhere — but when you persevere and succeed, you will experience a rare pleasure and pride every time you wear them. You may even find, as I do, that strangers can't resist the urge to come take a closer look and comment!

The secret to getting the pearls you really want is to look for intense luster and orient: *the more intense the luster and orient, the less noticeable all other factors become!*

This is easy to understand if you think about it for a moment; lustrousness actually creates an optical illusion making subtle differences less noticeable —

- *A slightly out-of-round pearl will look ROUNDER* because of the optical illusion created by its radiating glow
- *Moderate surface blemishes are LESS NOTICEABLE* because of the optical illusion created by its radiating glow
- *Color differences are MUTED* by the rainbow-like iridescence that pearls with good orient exhibit across their surface
- *Pearls look LARGER* because their glow emanates outward. Compare smaller pearls with intense luster and orient against larger pearls that are duller or chalkier. You'll see that the smaller, lustrous pearls will appear larger than the smaller ones!

Whatever type of pearl you choose — saltwater, freshwater, round, baroque, button, white, black, cream or gold — you'll have something wonderful as long as you choose a pearl with rich luster and iridescence.

Choosing Wisely

When buying pearls, it's important to take the time to compare various types, sizes, and qualities to develop an eye for the differences. Be sure to visit fine jewelers who are most likely to have a wide selection of pearl types and qualities. Here are some suggestions you might find helpful:

- **Compare the quality factors as you shop.** Pay special attention to differences in luster and orient as you compare other factors — color/tint, cleanliness, roundness, and size. You can learn a great deal about pearl quality simply by looking. Keeping each quality factor in mind as you compare, you may find roundness may be poor; if luster and color are good, they may not have clean surfaces; shape may be good but matching in the strand may be poor. And so on.

- **Examine pearls against your own neck and face** to be sure the color of the pearls suits your skin, eye and hair coloring.

- **Compare different sizes.** As you shop, ask what size the pearls are, and compare differences in cost for the same *quality*, in different sizes. A *double* strand of smaller pearls may cost less than a single strand of larger pearls, and create an equally important look.

To help develop an eye for subtle differences, it is sometimes helpful to ask to see the same *size* pearl, but at different prices. If you compare several different strands that are all the same size, but different prices, the variable will be *quality*; careful comparison can help you develop greater skill in spotting differences that affect cost.

- **Ask whether or not the color is** *natural* especially when considering colored pearls (gray, blue, black, golden, green, pink, etc.). Pearls of natural color often sell for much more than white pearls, whereas artificially colored pearls should sell for much less. If the color is natural, be sure it is so stated on the bill of sale.

- **Be sure to ask whether or not the pearls are genuine or simulated**, and be sure that "genuine *cultured*" or "genuine *natural*" is in writing on the bill of sale. Don't be afraid to use the "tooth test"; it won't harm the pearls (but remove lipstick first).

Shopping around can be of tremendous help before you buy pearls. It will help you become familiar with the wide range of pearls available within your price range; it will also develop your eye to distinguish quality differences, and help you decide what color, size, shape, and type are best for you. If you take the time to follow this advice, your pearls will be a source of lasting pleasure and pride.

Chapter 8

Pearl Choices — A World of Variety

Never before have there been so many beautiful pearl choices, from so many different parts of the world. In addition to Japan, where the art of culturing pearls was developed and refined, beautiful cultured pearls are being produced in many other countries including Australia, China, the Cook Islands, Indonesia, the Philippines, and Tahiti. Other countries that may become important sources for cultured pearls — some of which were once known for natural pearls — include India, Mexico, Thailand, Venezuela, Vietnam, and in the United States, Hawaii.

While pearls have certain characteristics in common no matter what their origin, each country or locality seems to produce a slightly different pearl, varying somewhat in color, orient and lustrousness, size or shape. Here we want to give you a glimpse of some of the wonderful pearls now available from major pearl-producing nations. The information and descriptions provided here will help you better understand the varieties now available, how they compare to each other, and what your choices are. (Color photographs begin following page **118**).

*Whatever the source, remember that **fine** pearls are produced in **every** country, and **poor** pearls are produced in **every** country.* When making a selection, the basic factors that affect quality must always be considered: luster and orient, color, surface perfection, shape, size, and in fancy-color pearls, tone.

Australia — The Best of "Down Under"

Australia is the world's largest producer of fine white South Sea pearls, producing round beauties that rival the finest that once came from Burma. The finest Australian pearls — large white pearls — are considered by many experts to be the "queen" of today's cultured pearl market. Australian "keshis" (see Chapter 4) are also very fine. They have become very desirable but are becoming increasingly rare.

- **Luster and orient.** Australian pearls offer a rich, subtle, satiny luster that is softer than that seen in Japanese Akoya pearls. While normally not quite as "silky" as the finest that once came from Burma, some of the finest now produced in Australia have been mistaken for Burmese.

- **Nacre thickness.** Very thick. Pearls are cultivated within the oyster for a much longer period of time than Chinese or Japanese varieties — up to three years. The resulting nacre coating is *much* thicker than that of other cultured saltwater pearls, 2-2.5 millimeters or more, and with proper care will provide lasting beauty and pleasure for many future generations.

- **Color.** Primarily in the white family, colors include white-pink (white with a pink blush), the rarest and most prized; silver-white, also highly prized; and warm creamy-pink. They also occur in blue, green gold and black tones.

- **Surface.** The rarest can be flawless, but as a result of the extensive length of time in the oyster, minor blemishes are often present. Generally speaking, minor blemishes are more acceptable in Australian pearls than in cultured pearls from China and Japan. As with all pearls, develop your own eye to see what is "normal" so you can better judge what is acceptable to you.

- **Shape.** Fine, round pearls are rarest. Australian cultured pearls are available in round and baroque shapes, symmetrical and asymmetrical.

- **Size.** Rarely smaller than 10 millimeters or over 20, which is exceptionally large and very rare in fine quality.

- **Treatments.** Minimal routine processing is the rule, and while some treatments such as dyeing have been reported, artificial enhancements are much less common. Australian producers have established very high standards and discourage dyeing and chemical treatments.

China —
Queen of the Freshwater Cultured Pearl

China has always been a land of contrasts, and so it is today with pearls. It is a land with vast potential, poised to become a world leader in the production of freshwater *and* saltwater varieties.

China now produces most of the world's freshwater cultured pearls and is producing a steadily increasing supply of saltwater cultured pearls.

- **Quality.** While there are fine, lustrous Chinese pearls available in a wide range of alluring colors and shapes at very affordable prices, low-quality pearls are also being produced in abundance. Quality varies dramatically, however, so it is virtually impossible to make general comparisons to similar varieties from Japan or other countries.

Saltwater cultured pearls. These include "Akoya" and "South Sea" types. The best Chinese Akoyas are under 6 millimeters in size; South Sea types are being produced in sizes over 10 millimeters. Quality varies widely, but generally speaking, Chinese Akoyas do not yet compare favorably with fine quality Japanese pearls in their lustrousness, orient, color, surface, shape or size; Chinese South Sea pearls are also normally inferior to those produced by other countries.

Freshwater cultured pearls. These include the "rice-krispie" type — narrow, elongated pearls with a crinkled surface — and somewhat larger, smoother "flat" varieties. The smoother, flatter types are often mistakenly compared to those from Japan's Lake Biwa, but in most cases cannot compare in shape, smoothness, and lustrousness.

Potato pearls are a bright spot in Chinese production. A wonderful new type of "*nucleated*" freshwater cultured pearl introduced by China, this creation is a near-round, **all-nacre** cultured pearl. It often resembles an oval "potato" in shape, which is how it got its nickname, and occurs in a wide range of colors, including white and pastel shades. While the exact technique used to produce these beauties is not known, we do know it involves implanting a round, *all-nacre nucleus,* perhaps made from a non-nucleated freshwater cultured pearl such as the inexpensive tissue-graft rice-krispie type, shaped into round beads after harvesting and then re-implanted in another freshwater mollusc. Whatever the case, the finest "potato" pearls are very beautiful, all-nacre pearls and exhibit a rich luster and orient rivalling a natural pearl. They are much less expensive than other round pearls and provide excellent value and long-lasting beauty; unfortunately, sizes rarely exceed 6 millimeters.

Chinese freshwater pearls occur in every color, size, and shape — including stick, cross, and wing shapes — and every quality. There is a huge range in quality, so be sure to compare carefully.

Pay special attention to the quality of the luster, surface, and shape. Also keep in mind that many Chinese fancy-color freshwater pearls have obtained their color from dye, and white pearls are routinely subjected to excessive processing.

- **Treatments.** Most of China's production is routinely bleached and dyed, and many pearls are subjected to extensive treatment.

The Cook Islands —
Aubergines to Whet Any Appetite

While similar to other natural color "black" pearls being cultured throughout French Polynesia, this newcomer to the world of cultured pearls is producing some of the most distinctive colors — sensual shades in mauve to aubergine. Designers are just discovering this lovely pearl, and "cooking" up some luscious creations!

- **Luster and orient.** Less bright and intense than Japanese pearls; subdued and velvety in character. Less intense luster and orient than Tahitian.

- **Nacre thickness.** Very thick; comparable to that of other cultured South Sea pearls.

- **Color.** While some silvery-gray to black shades are produced with overtones typical of other locations in French Polynesia, most exhibit a distinctive bronze to dark gray-brown body color with strong pink overtones. The resulting "dusty rose," "mauve" and "aubergine" shades are very appealing and distinctive.

  Black pearls are currently being produced throughout French Polynesia in about 30 lagoons. Each lagoon produces pearls with slightly varying color characteristics (because of differences in the water itself). The pearls coming from the Cook Islands are produced in just two lagoons, so many of the pearls are very similar in color. For this reason, when one says "Cook Island" pearls, a particular shade of color in the rose-bronze category now comes to mind — mauve, dusty rose, aubergine. While very lovely, they are not considered the premier color, so they are considered less valuable than Tahitian blacks.

- **Quality.** Quality overall, in terms of shape, surface perfection and luster, is inferior to Tahitian cultured pearls. Nonetheless, the finer Cook Island pearls are very lovely and can make an excellent choice at an affordable cost. Avoid low-luster pearls.

- **Size.** Rarely under 8 millimeters, but the largest sizes are normally smaller than those being produced in Tahiti.

- **Treatments.** No bleaching, dyeing, or artificial enhancements; minimal routine processing only.

Indonesia and the Philippines — A Golden Future in South Sea Cultured Pearls

Indonesia and the Philippines have created more than a ripple with their exotic creamy, yellow and golden pearls; in fact, they've created a wave!

For many years, the more traditional "white" pearl was clearly preferred to warm cream or yellow colors. That has changed. As pearl buyers have become more sophisticated, and conformity is no longer the rule, color has moved centerstage. Fine quality cultured pearls from Indonesia and the Philippines are a wonderful choice for anyone who likes "warm" tones.

Here is a glimpse of the exotic, tranquil character of the Philippine cultured pearl. [We regret that Indonesia, which has produced some magnificent deep-gold pearls — as well as some lovely, if somewhat spotted, pink pearls — has suffered a major setback following a series of catastrophic natural disasters and production has been greatly reduced. For this reason, we are focusing on the Philippine pearl here, but barring any further setbacks, the near future looks very exciting for Indonesia.]

- **Quality.** Philippine pearls are produced by white-lipped oysters as in other South Sea areas, and by a *yellow-lipped* oyster which can produce rich, deep, dark gold. They are similar in quality to other South Sea pearls — softer luster with good orient, and thicker nacre than Chinese and Japanese cultured pearls, with a wide range of shapes and surface perfection. The overall size is also larger than Japanese and Chinese cultured pearls and comparable to other South Sea pearls *(Indonesian pearls are normally smaller than other South Sea pearls and often comparable to large Akoyas. In smaller sizes the Indonesian South Sea pearl is an attractive thick-nacre alternative to large Akoyas)*. They should be evaluated as any other pearl. **Beware of *three-quarter* pearls sold as *round*.**

- **Color** is the distinctive feature of Philippine and Indonesian pearls, although Indonesia is also beginning to produce some very white pearls in the smaller size range (10-11 mm). Ranging from a distinctive cream, sometimes with a strong yellow cast, to a rich, deep gold, these colorful pearls can be a striking complement to tan and tawny complexions. The richer the color, the rarer. A fine "fancy" deep-golden pearl can be more costly than a comparable white-pink South Sea cultured pearl; pale yellow or yellow-cream is less rare and costs less than comparable whites.

In evaluating color, keep in mind that you must develop your eye to learn what is most pleasing to you as well as what colors are most rare and costly, or least rare and most affordable. In addition to "body color" and "overtone," remember that the "tone" — how light or dark the color appears — is particularly important in evaluating pearls in the yellow range; a shade of difference in tone can dramatically affect price. REMEMBER: *When comparing fancy-color pearls, view them in the same type of light whenever possible* since their color will look different when viewed in daylight, indoor fluorescent light, incandescent light, or spotlight.

Japan — Home of "Akoya" and "Biwa" Cultured Pearls

Japan's *Akoya* pearl is for most people the "pearl of pearls" — magnificent, lustrous, round, and white! While the finest Japanese cultured pearls are very costly, especially in sizes over 8 millimeters, they are much more affordable than the larger and even costlier South Sea pearls (which most can only dream about).

In the freshwater category, Japan's "Biwa" pearl (from Lake Biwa) set the standard for freshwater cultured pearls for many years. However, as a result of ecological requirements to protect the lake's shore, production has now ceased almost entirely. [Many freshwater cultured pearls from China are now sent to Japan and sold as "Biwa" but they are not the same type of pearl, nor do they look like the true Biwa.] Since few Biwa pearls are now available, Japan's Akoya cultured pearls are our focus here.

- **Luster and orient.** Fine Akoyas can *exhibit the most intense luster of any white round, saltwater cultured pearl.* Look for pearls with high luster and avoid those with low luster, indicating thin nacre. When nacre is thick, you may also see the prized, soft iridescence we call "orient" as you turn the pearl (as you "orient" it).

  Buy the best quality you can afford, but never accept low luster. Insist on a lustrous pearl, even if this means the shape may be slightly off or the surface somewhat spotted.

- **Nacre thickness.** The nacre coating is less thick on Akoya cultured pearls than on the South Sea types, and the thickness can vary from one producer to another. Overall, however, it is thicker than most Chinese Akoyas, and very thick nacre can be found in the very finest cultured Japanese pearls. Nacre thickness generally averages less than

0.4 millimeters in very round pearls, and may be as low as 0.2 millimeters or less. The finest can measure 1.0 millimeter in thickness (on each side of a round pearl, equalling 2 millimeters of *total* diameter), and in rare cases, *over* one millimeter.

- **Color.** Normally in the white family. The rarest is white with a surface blush of pink; cream shades are also pleasing, and can be very beautiful; those with a slight greenish overtone cost less but can be very lovely against certain complexions. Overall, "white" Japanese pearls tend to be whiter than the Chinese. Occasionally pearls occur in unusual colors including pink, blue, gold and gray. Japan is also producing a natural color "black" pearl, which, while smaller than those produced in French Polynesia, is also produced by the "black-lip" oyster and is similar in appearance.

- **Shape.** Japanese cultured pearls occur in many shapes including round and baroque; symmetrical and asymmetrical. Rounder than the Chinese, Japanese Akoya pearls are typically more round than all other pearls. Remember, however, that "roundness" is not necessarily an indication of a fine pearl — *cultured pearls with very thin nacre are always very round* because they haven't been inside the oyster long enough to become misshapen. So when selecting round Akoya pearls, be sure to select pearls with very high luster.

  Baroque Akoya pearls are also very desirable — and much more affordable than round — especially in teardrop or other distinctive shapes showing strong iridescence. Sometimes they resemble flowers or animals, truly unique creations of nature's exclusive making!

- **Size.** The range is 2 to 12 millimeters in diameter, although they rarely exceed 10 millimeters. There is a dramatic jump in cost after $7\frac{1}{2}$ millimeters. The price jumps upward rapidly with each half-millimeter from 8 millimeters up. Production of Japanese pearls is shifting away from sizes under 6 millimeters, focusing on sizes from 6-8+ millimeters.

- **Treatments.** The finest receive only minimal routine processing, but some are subjected to excessive treatments including chemical bleaching, tumbling and dyeing.

Tahiti — Black Pearls of Paradise

Few things rival Tahiti when it comes to exotic beauty and romance, and this holds equally true for its pearls — naturally "black" Tahitian cultured pearls are among the most sought after and treasured of all gems. The world famous jewelry firm of Harry Winston in New

York knew it the moment they saw the first strands ever to come from Tahiti, and they bought them all...twenty strands! That was in 1978. Today, the cultured pearls of Tahiti set the world standard for black pearls.

Most "black pearls" are in the "gray" range, but the term "black" is used to refer to the overall type produced by a large *black*-lipped oyster. This particular oyster — which measures about 12 inches at maturity — produces a dark nacre that is responsible for the unusual colors seen in this variety. Be careful not to confuse "natural" black pearls with *natural* pearls; in this case, only the *color* is "natural"; the pearl is *cultured*. (Natural black, *natural* pearls also occur. These are rare and are typically a less intense, less desirable black-to-bronze color).

- **Luster and orient.** The lustrousness is normally more subdued than in other varieties, almost velvety, but they can also exhibit luster so intense that it resembles the metallic sheen of a ballbearing. Strong iridescence is characteristic, and helps to create the exotic character seen in many of these pearls.

- **Nacre thickness.** Very thick (averaging about 2 millimeters in relation to the total diameter) as a result of a two to three year cultivation period in the oyster.

- **Color.** The colors are dramatic and range from light "dove" gray to a medium-deep "gunmetal" gray. Other colors include the rare "peacock" (a vivid green with magenta overtone), "eggplant" (magenta with a green overtone), green, olive-green, blue, magenta, and occasionally "seafoam" green (a silvery green with a pale blue overtone). The browner, bronzier shades are less costly, but can still be very pleasing.

  The color in the Tahitian black pearl is often not uniform throughout. The pearl can be black on one end, and much lighter on the other end; there can be subtle gradations from one part of the pearl to another. This also adds to their dramatic appearance and allure. Each is individual. The more uniform the color, the rarer and, in most cases, the costlier.

- **Surface.** Virtually flawless surfaces are exceptionally rare. Minor blemishes are characteristic, but given the darker color of these pearls, they are usually less noticeable, even when somewhat extensive. Most naturally black cultured pearls will exhibit small surface imperfections that can be noticed with close scrutiny; pearls with large, clearly visible imperfections may still be attractive, but should cost less. You must take time to examine a wide selection of Tahitian pearls to develop your own eye to recognize what is or is not acceptable.

- **Shape.** Perfectly round pearls are exceptionally rare, and even rarer in fine quality (again, as a result of the longer-than-average cultivation period inside the oyster). Other shapes to consider are near-round, button, teardrop, and the increasingly popular Tahitian "ringed" pearl (see Chapter 4) which is very affordable and very popular with leading jewelry designers.

- **Size.** Rarely less than 8 millimeters, the average size is 10-12 millimeters; 14-17 millimeters is considered very large, and these are rare. In fine quality, a *single* pearl over 14 millimeters is very rare and very costly; a matched strand is exceptionally rare and exceptionally costly.

- **Treatments.** Minimal routine processing; no bleaching, dyeing or artificial enhancements as part of routine processing.

    Occasionally off-color South Sea and Tahitian pearls are artificially colored black through dyeing, exposure to radiation, or silver nitrate solution, and sold as "natural black." While not common, these continue to surface from time to time. For this reason, and in light of their very high cost, when buying fine black pearls we recommend obtaining a laboratory report confirming "natural" color if they are represented as such.

    With so many variations in color and shape, we recommend visiting several fine jewelers before selecting any Tahitian cultured pearl to be sure you have viewed a wide enough selection to make a choice that best meets your personal taste and desires.

United States —
A Bold New Look in Pearls

It should come as little surprise that the "new world" — the land known for modern innovation — would be the land to give birth to a daring new type of pearl: the American freshwater cultured pearl. There is no other pearl quite like this American beauty, produced exclusively on pearl farms in the waters of Tennessee (see Chapter 4). Look for unusual baroque and fancy shapes; if considering a "mabé," American freshwater *solid blister pearls* such as the domé® make attractive, much more durable alternatives.

- **Luster and orient.** Intensely high luster and rich orient.

- **Nacre thickness.** The thickest nacre of any cultured pearl in relationship to the size of the nucleus.

- **Color.** Wide range of neutral colors including white, silver, gray, cream; natural fancy colors in pink, peach, and lavender shades.

- **Surface.** Virtually flawless surfaces are exceptionally rare as a result of remaining in the mollusc so much longer than any other cultured pearl; minor blemishes are more likely to be present, and are more acceptable than in other cultured pearls.

- **Shape.** Predominantly baroque and "fancy shapes" including bars, drops, pears, coins, ovals, navettes, marquises, and cabochons. Round, heart, and teardrop shapes are available in solid blister-type. [Round pearls are available in limited quantity, but dramatically increased cultivation efforts now promise much greater availability in the near future.]

- **Size.** Ranges widely depending upon shape; can be as small as a 9 by 11 millimeter cabochon, or as large as 40 by 10 millimeters.

- **Treatments.** Routine *cleaning* only. No bleaching, dyeing, or artificial enhancements.

Chapter 9

Pearl Prices — Some Guidelines

Comparing prices is always a complex issue for which most people seek a simple solution. Many would like to have a simple list of pearl types and prices, by quality and size. Unfortunately, with market conditions constantly changing, and without a universally accepted quality grading system, this is not possible.

But this does not mean we cannot provide some general guidelines that will help you understand how different types of pearls compare to one another in terms of cost, and how size and quality can affect pricing.

The following charts are not intended as price lists of what you should be paying in a jewelry store; they should be used, instead, as a guideline and foundation from which to make sounder price comparisons.

American Cultured Freshwater Pearls

Coin

Prices are per each

	Fine	Very Fine	Gem
10.5x4 mm	$16.00-32.00	$40.00-53.00	$65.00
12.5x4 mm	$21.00-42.00	$50.00-63.00	$80.00

Bar

Prices are per each

	Fine	Very Fine	Gem
15.2-16x3-3.5 mm	$9.00-20.00	$35.00	$45.00
16-17x3.5-4 mm	$16.00-20.00	$45.00	$55.00
20x9.5x7 mm	$80.00	$150.00	$200.00

Flat Drop

Prices are per each

	Fine	Very Fine	Gem
17.5x8x5.5 mm	$19.00-42.00	$50.00	$78.00

Navette

Prices are per each

	Fine	Very Fine	Gem
24.5x7x4.5 mm	$25.00-35.00	$56.00	$70.00

Matched pairs are approximately 10% higher. Natural colors harder to match.
No bleaches, dyes, or enhancements are used. Sizes are approximate within 1mm.

Prices adjusted to retail. Source: "The Guide," Gemworld International, Inc., Northbrook, Illinois

Cultured Saltwater Pearl Necklaces

Choker (16" length) / Princess (18" length)

With 14K clasp, prices are per strand

	Commercial 1-4 B	Good 4-6 A	Fine 6-8 AA	Extra Fine 8-10 AAA
2-2.5mm 16"	$240-380	$380-580	$580-800	$800-1,000
2.5-3mm 16"	$220-330	$330-550	$550-770	$770-990
3-3.5mm 16"	$220-330	$330-550	$550-770	$770-990
3.5-4mm 16"	$200-320	$320-490	$490-590	$590-850
4-4.5mm 16"	$200-340	$340-530	$530-650	$650-910
4.5-5mm 16"	$210-370	$370-570	$570-790	$790-1,190
5-5.5mm 16"	$240-390	$390-630	$630-990	$990-1,430
5.5-6mm 16"	$260-400	$400-690	$690-1,050	$1,050-1,700
6-6.5mm 18"	$330-500	$500-880	$880-1,450	$1,450-1,900
6.5-7mm 18"	$370-590	$590-1,100	$1,100-1,700	$1,700-2,800
7-7.5mm 18"	$450-710	$710-1,300	$1,300-2,600	$2,600-4,000
7.5-8mm 18"	$700-1,100	$1,100-2,500	$2,500-4,600	$4,600-8,000
8-8.5mm 18"	$750-1,450	$1,450-3,100	$3,100-6,800	$6,800-10,000
8.5-9mm 18"	$980-1,800	$1,800-4,200	$4,200-8,400	$8,400-12,600
9-9.5mm 18"	$2,200-4,400	$4,400-9,200	$9,200-16,200	$16,200-25,500
9.5-10mm 18"	$2,600-8,000	$8,000-16,000	$16,000-29,000	$29,000-42,000

Note: Some manufacturers may produce 5-5.5mm and 5.5-6mm in 18" length.
Add on for the additional length.

Prices adjusted to retail. Source: "The Guide," Gemworld International, Inc., Northbrook, Illinois

Cultured Saltwater Pearl Necklaces

Matinee (24" to 27" length)

With 14K clasp, prices are per strand

	Commercial 1-4 B	Good 4-6 A	Fine 6-8 AA	Extra Fine 8-10 AAA
2-2.5mm 24"	$360-570	$570-870	$870-1,200	$1,200-1,500
2.5-3mm 24"	$330-500	$500-830	$830-1,160	$1,160-1,490
3-3.5mm 24"	$330-500	$500-830	$830-1,160	$1,160-1,490
3.5-4mm 24"	$300-480	$480-740	$740-890	$890-1,280
4-4.5mm 24"	$300-510	$510-800	$800-980	$980-1,370
4.5-5mm 24"	$320-560	$560-860	$860-1,190	$1,190-1,790
5-5.5mm 24"	$360-570	$570-950	$950-1,490	$1,490-2,150
5.5-6mm 24"	$390-600	$600-1,040	$1,040-1,580	$1,580-2,550
6-6.5mm 27"	$500-750	$750-1,320	$1,320-2,180	$2,180-2,850
6.5-7mm 27"	$560-890	$890-1,650	$1,650-2,550	$2,550-4,200
7-7.5mm 27"	$680-1,070	$1,070-1,950	$1,950-3,900	$3,900-6,000
7.5-8mm 27"	$1,050-1,650	$1,650-3,750	$3,750-6,900	$6,900-12,000
8-8.5mm 27"	$1,130-2,180	$2,180-4,650	$4,650-10,200	$10,200-15,000
8.5-9mm 27"	$1,470-2,700	$2,700-6,300	$6,300-12,600	$12,600-18,900
9-9.5mm 27"	$3,300-6,600	$6,600-13,800	$13,800-24,300	$24,300-38,250
9.5-10mm 27"	$3,900-12,000	$12,000-24,000	$24,000-43,500	$43,500-63,000

Prices adjusted to retail. Source: "The Guide," Gemworld International, Inc., Northbrook, Illinois

Cultured Saltwater Pearl Necklaces

Opera (32" to 36" length)

With 14K clasp, prices are per strand

	Commercial 1-4 B	Good 4-6 A	Fine 6-8 AA	Extra Fine 8-10 AAA
2-2.5mm 32"	$480-760	$760-1,160	$1,160-1,600	$1,600-2,000
2.5-3mm 32"	$440-660	$660-1,100	$1,100-1,540	$1,540-1,980
3-3.5mm 32"	$440-660	$660-1,100	$1,110-1,540	$1,540-1,980
3.5-4mm 32"	$400-640	$640-980	$980-1,180	$1,180-1,700
4-4.5mm 32"	$400-680	$680-1,060	$1,060-1,300	$1,300-1,820
4.5-5mm 32"	$420-740	$740-1,140	$1,140-1,580	$1,580-2,380
5-5.5mm 32"	$480-760	$760-1,260	$1,260-1,980	$1,980-2,860
5.5-6mm 32"	$520-800	$800-1,380	$1,380-2,100	$2,100-3,400
6-6.5mm 36"	$660-1,000	$1,000-1,760	$1,760-2,900	$2,900-3,800
6.5-7mm 36"	$740-1,180	$1,180-2,200	$2,200-3,400	$3,400-5,600
7-7.5mm 36"	$900-1,420	$1,420-2,600	$2,600-5,200	$5,200-8,000
7.5-8mm 36"	$1,400-2,200	$2,200-5,000	$5,000-9,200	$9,200-16,000
8-8.5mm 36"	$1,500-2,900	$2,900-6,200	$6,200-13,600	$16,600-20,000
8.5-9mm 36"	$1,960-3,600	$3,600-8,400	$8,400-16,800	$16,800-25,200
9-9.5mm 36"	$4,400-8,800	$8,800-18,400	$18,400-32,400	$32,400-51,000
9.5-10mm 36"	$5,200-16,000	$16,000-32,000	$32,000-58,000	$58,000-84,000

Prices adjusted to retail. Source: "The Guide," Gemworld International, Inc., Northbrook, Illinois

Cultured Saltwater Pearl Necklaces

Graduated (19" length)

With 14K clasp, prices are per strand
Smaller pearls at ends to larger pearls in middle

	Commercial 1-4 B	Good 4-6 A	Fine 6-8 AA	Extra Fine 8-10 AAA
3x7mm	$300-420	$420-750	$750-950	$950-1,500
4x8mm	$380-460	$460-820	$820-1,250	$1,250-1,800

Baroque Cultured Saltwater Pearl Necklaces

Choker (16" length) / Princess (18" length)

With 14K clasp, prices are per strand

	Commercial 1-4 B	Good 4-6 A	Fine 6-8 AA	Extra Fine 8-10 AAA
5.5-6mm	$110-160	$160-280	$280-400	$400-460
6-6.5mm	$140-200	$200-380	$380-460	$460-530
6.5-7mm	$160-220	$220-400	$400-520	$520-600
7-7.5mm	$180-230	$230-500	$500-800	$800-920
7.5-8mm	$280-310	$310-600	$600-1,040	$1,040-1,200
8-8.5mm	$320-360	$360-750	$750-1,200	$1,200-1,380
8.5-9mm	$370-430	$430-900	$900-1,380	$1,380-1,590
9-9.5mm	$690-800	$800-1,500	$1,500-3,450	$3,450-3,970
9.5-10mm	$1,150-1,730	$1,730-3,400	$3,400-4,600	$4,600-5,290

Prices adjusted to retail. Source: "The Guide," Gemworld International, Inc., Northbrook, Illinois

South Sea Cultured Pearls

Prices are per pearl

	Commercial (Baroque) 1-4 B	Good 4-6 A	Fine 6-8 AA	Extra Fine 8-10 AAA
10mm-11mm	$600-1,200	$1,200-2,500	$2,500-3,300	$3,300-5,500
11mm-12mm	$850-1,150	$1,150-2,600	$2,600-3,700	$3,700-5,950
12mm-13mm	$1,200-1,600	$1,600-3,000	$3,000-4,300	$4,300-6,600
13mm-14mm	$1,450-2,650	$2,650-4,200	$4,200-5,500	$5,500-7,700
14mm-14.5mm	$1,800-3,400	$3,400-5,500	$5,500-8,200	$8,200-12,400
14.5mm-15mm	$2,250-4,200	$4,200-8,200	$8,200-12,400	$12,400-18,000
15mm-15.5mm	$3,400-7,000	$7,000-12,000	$12,000-16,400	$16,400-22,000

Freshwater Rice Pearl Necklaces

Choker (16" length) / Princess (18" length)

Unstrung, prices are per strand

	Commercial	Good	Fine
3-3.5mm	$2.00-3.00	$3.00-4.00	$4.00-6.00
3.5-4mm	$3.00-4.00	$4.00-6.00	$6.00-12.00
4-5mm	$4.00-5.00	$5.00-7.00	$7.00-20.00

Prices adjusted to retail. Source: "The Guide," Gemworld International, Inc., Northbrook, Illinois

Mabé Pearls

Prices are per pearl
Good to fine quality only

Rounds	
10mm	$100
11mm	$110
12mm	$120
13mm	$130
14mm	$140
15mm	$170
16mm	$180-240
17mm	$220-390
18mm	$280-400
19mm	$330-500
20mm	$450-650

Pear Shape	
12-14mm	$150
14-15mm	$180-220
16-18mm	$300-350

Prices adjusted to retail. Source: "The Guide," Gemworld International, Inc., Northbrook, Illinois

Tahitian Black Cultured Pearls

Round

Prices are per pearl

	Commercial or C	Good or B	Good + or B+	Fine or A
up to 8mm	$150-230	$230-300	$300-370	$370-450
8-8.5mm	$200-240	$240-400	$400-510	$510-680
8.5-9mm	$230-400	$400-520	$520-700	$700-900
9-9.5mm	$290-520	$520-730	$730-1,000	$1,000-1,280
9.5-10mm	$400-540	$540-1,000	$1,000-1,350	$1,350-1,800
10-10.5mm	$470-950	$950-1,500	$1,500-1,950	$1,950-2,400
10.5-11mm	$600-850	$850-2,000	$2,000-2,400	$2,400-3,150
11-11.5mm	$850-1,850	$1,850-2,900	$2,900-3,650	$3,650-4,300
11.5-12mm	$1,850-3,200	$3,200-3,700	$3,700-4,150	$4,150-5,100

Sizes larger than 12mm and necklaces are negotiable.
Matched pairs are approximately 10% higher.

Prices adjusted to retail. Source: "The Guide," Gemworld International, Inc., Northbrook, Illinois

Tahitian Black Cultured Pearls

Drop or Button

Prices are per pearl

	Commercial or C	Good or B	Good + or B+	Fine or A
up to 8mm	$130-190	$190-250	$250-310	$310-380
8-8.5mm	$190-240	$240-340	$340-490	$490-630
8.5-9mm	$200-270	$370-510	$510-670	$670-850
9-9.5mm	$280-390	$390-730	$730-920	$920-1,160
9.5-10mm	$340-500	$500-970	$970-1,200	$1,200-1,420
10-10.5mm	$370-600	$600-1,250	$1,250-1,660	$1,660-2,000
10.5-11mm	$550-900	$900-1,850	$1,850-2,200	$2,200-2,550
11-11.5mm	$730-1,700	$1,700-2,450	$2,450-3,150	$3,150-3,750
11.5-12mm	$1,220-2,450	$2,450-3,550	$3,550-4,000	$4,000-4,850

Sizes larger than 12mm and necklaces are negotiable.
Matched pairs are approximately 10% higher.

Prices adjusted to retail. Source: "The Guide," Gemworld International, Inc., Northbrook, Illinois

Tahitian Black Cultured Pearls

Circlés

Prices are per pearl

	Commercial or C	Good or B	Fine or A
up to 8mm	$70-100	$100-130	$130-170
8-9mm	$120-140	$140-170	$170-220
9-10mm	$150-200	$200-220	$220-270
10-11mm	$200-260	$260-320	$320-350
11-12mm	$240-320	$320-400	$400-500

Sizes larger than 12mm and necklaces are negotiable.
Matched pairs are approximately 10% higher.

Baroque

Prices are per pearl

up to 9mm	$110-130
9-10mm	$160-200
over 10mm	$270-320

Prices adjusted to retail. Source: "The Guide," Gemworld International, Inc., Northbrook, Illinois

Part Five
Lustrous Advice from Illustrious Experts

Chapter 10

The Experts Speak

Here you will find advice from leading experts and producers from each country — internationally recognized authorities — who were specially selected and invited to comment here. Interspersed throughout this chapter you will find their responses — interesting personal recollections and anecdotes, general advice on selecting pearls, and some unusual "insider buying tips." These comments reflect their own points of view, based on years of experience in culturing and selling pearls. They are entertaining as well as practical (and we hope you'll heed advice that reoccurs from one expert to the other — after all, these are people who are really "in the know"!).

We think you will find this chapter especially helpful in gaining a better understanding of what your choices are.

Eve J. Alfillé
Eve J. Alfillé Gallery (United States)

The Eve J. Alfillé Gallery is one of the leading designer jewelry galleries in the United States, known especially for their use of pearls of every variety and color. Alfillé was formerly on the Board of the International Pearl Association and is the Founder and Director of The International Pearl Society, an organization for pearl connoisseurs.

Alfillé on Lustrous Ways to Be Distinctive

"Pay more attention to distinctive *shapes*. We've been 'sold' on round pearls because that's what we're being offered and, for most jewelers, it's a safe bet. "I love irregularly shaped pearls, especially large baroque and keshi pearls, freshwater pearls from Lake Biwa, American freshwater pearls, and abalone pearls. First, each is truly unique and offers wonderful possibilities for creating the most interesting and distinctive pieces of jewelry. And even more important, these pearls exhibit an especially rich luster and shimmering iridescent orient that sets them apart and adds a dimension to their beauty that many pearls lack."

Colors Other Than White Can Create Any Mood

"Pay more attention to unusual or subtle colors. We have been brainwashed into thinking we must all wear white or pink-white pearls, yet brunettes, for example, look even more beautiful in subtle ivory or creamy tones. In Europe these creamier colors command a premium, while in the U.S., they are more affordable. Baroque, keshi, Biwa, American freshwater, and some of the new Chinese freshwater pearls offer these lovely shades and, in addition, a wide range of distinctive hues such as lavender, peach, blue, rose, green, gold, and gray. The right color, in the right design, can enhance any mood you wish to create — soft and feminine, quiet and demure, or secretly sensual. They also look lovely combined with colored gemstones. But to see such colors, you will have to find a jeweler who loves and specializes in pearls."

Salvador Assael
Assael International (United States)

Salvador Assael is the Chairman of Assael International, an international firm known for its rare and costly gems. Assael is also a cultured pearl producer as well as one of the leading importers of fine natural black cultured pearls from Tahiti, and white cultured South Sea pearls. A major influence in the very development of the cultured pearl industry for almost 50 years, he is also President of the Tahitian Black Pearl Promotion Association for the Americas, and sits on the Board of the South Sea Pearl Consortium.

A Priceless Pearl Story from Assael

"If only my mind and memory could recall all the incredible pearls, natural and cultured, that have gone through my hands, I would need not one page to describe them, but fifty. The most memorable, however, was a relatively recent experience, and it is quite a story.

"In 1986, while sorting our newly arrived white pearl crop, we discovered one incredible, enormous 'button' pearl that measured approximately 24 millimeters in diameter. Its shape was exquisitely beautiful, but its color was indescribably awful — without question the most distasteful we'd ever seen in a pearl. Nonetheless, we had to price it, although we weren't sure how to go about it. None of the staff, including myself, had any idea of its value, but we finally decided it was worth $3,000 simply for its rare size and shape.

"But suddenly, as I turned the pearl around, I saw several overlapping layers in the back, and sheer curiosity made me begin to peel* the layers at that particular spot. I noticed a big opening in one of the center layers; was it possible that something more beautiful lay beneath the surface? To make a long story short, we finally decided to peel the pearl. It was a gamble. On one hand, we risked destroying what we already had, but on the other hand, we might find something quite different underneath.

"We proceeded. We were hopeful and we were intrigued; but we were also dubious and wondered if we were being foolish. Peeling away the surface is risky: it can as easily reveal something worse as something better (but is this not also the case in life?). And then, there it was. Beneath the deceptive surface lay something more exquisite than we ever imagined...*here was one of the rarest, most magnificent pink pearls ever revealed!* We quietly gazed upon an exquisitely shaped, spotless, lustrous pink pearl measuring 22 millimeters! I have never seen or handled, before or since, a pearl of that size, quality, or beauty. Few pearls are as desirable as this one was. It was immediately acquired — for $100,000 — by a 'great Lady of Society' who found it irresistible (or so we were told by the jeweler who sold it)!

"This is one of my favorite stories because, although about a pearl, it is so true of people, and life. But then I often find with pearls, more than with any other gem, endless parables for life itself. It is just another of the reasons I am especially drawn to them."

On the Symbolism of the
Exotic Black Cultured Pearl

"Here, as nature would have it, we do not find the soft white pearl, but pearls suggestive of passion, of swirling emotions beneath the surface, and of the beauty that can result from many different colors mingling together in rich harmony. The black pearl of Polynesia captures the rainbow after the storm. It is a symbol of hope for all humanity."

---

*Peeling the layers of a pearl is an ancient, dying art; there are only a handful of pearl experts in the world that still know how to perform this ancient technique.

On the World's Largest Black Cultured Pearl

"The *Pinctada margaritifera*, the black-lipped oyster that produces the natural black color cultured pearl, produces large pearls so it is not unusual to harvest some that are unusually large. However, large *round* pearls (over 18 millimeters) are *very* rare from this oyster species, and rarer still in fine quality. So you can imagine our surprise when, in 1994, from an oyster cultivated in the Marutea lagoon in Tahiti, came a 19 millimeter, perfectly round pearl, of exceptional quality. This is the largest round black cultured pearl ever harvested, and one which we now own."

Jacques Branellec
Jewelmer International Corporation
(Philippines)

Jacques Branellec is the Chairman of Jewelmer. Founded by him in 1979 with partner Manuel Cojuangco, Jewelmer is the leading producer of South Sea pearls in the Philippines today. Jacques Branellec has been actively involved in cultivating, harvesting and marketing cultured pearls for almost 30 years.

Branellec on Getting What You Really Want

"Pearls are evaluated subjectively. Unlike diamonds, which can be precisely graded according to a universally accepted system, pearls must be judged subjectively for the most part. Orient and luster are the two most important factors to learn to judge. If these are rich and beautiful, all else can be left to personal preference and financial considerations.

"When buying pearls, go to a jeweler who *issues a certificate of authenticity*, confirming genuineness and natural color. It is also very important to buy from a knowledgeable retailer with extensive pearl expertise. Keep in mind that not all retailers are knowledgeable about pearls, and differences in their quality and value (this is especially true of 'peddlers' on the streets of pearl-producing countries). You must search for jewelers who really understand pearls and how to evaluate them; this is your best assurance that you will get good quality pearls.

"Just as wine connoisseurs know where their wine comes from, know where your pearls come from. Be sure your jeweler obtains pearls directly from the producer or from a reputable importer; this will help to ensure that representations made are accurate."

Bartholomew D'Elia
B. D'Elia & Son, Inc. (United States)

Bartholomew D'Elia is President of B. D'Elia & Son, Inc., a firm specializing in pearls founded by his great-grandfather in 1856. D'Elia has over 40 years experience as a pearl importer and supplier, having begun his career in 1948 learning all about cultivating, processing and selection on a pearl farm in Japan (at which time he was one of only four Americans living in all of Japan, and his company was the only American pearl company with an office there).

D'Elia — The Man Who Acquired Mikimoto's
Personal Collection — Tells How It Happened!

"It was 1948. I was 26 and living in Tokyo for a time to learn about pearls. The war was over and the Japanese and Americans were forging an economic bond that would have far-reaching consequences. At that time the Japanese government was trying to break up the huge pearl cartel and had set up the CILC — Closed Institutions Liquidating Committee. All pearls were to be turned over to the CILC and then sold at auction. So, at the same time I was trying to establish myself and continue the D'Elia line of leadership in pearls, the Japanese pearl industry was having to face the problem of product liquidation.

"At 2:00 a.m. the night before I was to leave to return home, I received a phone call. 'Who is it?' I asked. 'Bart,' the voice at the other end said. 'The old man wants to see you. I can't talk about it on the phone, but I know it's an opportunity you won't want to pass up. Be at the island tomorrow.' He hung up.

D'Elia with Mikimoto

"The 'old man' was Kokichi Mikimoto, at 89 years of age, the legendary pioneer in the development of Japanese pearl culture. He had known my father and grandfather, and he was a good friend. The 'island' was his famous pearl farm, where he lived and produced some of the finest cultured pearls in the world. I sensed there was something very important here. Something that comes along once in a lifetime, so I cancelled my trip home and went to Mikimoto's Toba island instead.

"The old man greeted me and took me into his little house. I noticed as I walked in that the floorboards were creaking in a strange way. We sat and talked awhile over a cup of tea. He said, 'You know, I turned over lots of pearls to the CILC,' and then he smiled. 'But I kept some for myself. And Bart, right now you're sitting on them.'

"I realized then that under the floorboards of Mikimoto's home was his own private stock, handpicked by the legendary pearl master himself. Then he turned to me and said, 'If you want to buy them, they're yours.' And so, I made a pearl purchase that comes along only once in a lifetime. It's one I'll never forget."

D'Elia on Pearl Quality Today and on Detrimental Treatments

"In recent years, very unfortunately, the raw material pearls ('hama-age' in Japanese — the pearls before they are processed) have deteriorated very drastically in quality. *This means that the first thing to look for is the cultivation on a pearl.* [Here D'Elia is referring to the quality and thickness of the nacre coating.] Naturally the shape and color are important, but this is also a matter of personal preference to some degree.

"The degree of processing and treatment to which the raw material pearl has been subjected is an area for concern. Quite frankly, overtreated pearls are very common today; and overtreated pearls do tend to lose color and even luster after treatment."

Dr. H.A. Hanni
Swiss Gemmological Institute (Switzerland)

Dr. H.A. Hanni, Director of the Swiss Gemmological Institute, is one of the world's premier gemologists and a leading research scientist in the gemological community. Situated in Europe, he has been privileged to examine some of the world's finest gems and jewels, many of royal descent. Thus he has had wide experience working with the finest natural as well as cultured pearls.

Hanni Compares the Factors
You Should Consider When Buying Pearls

"First, a word on pearl reports. Nacre thickness on cultured pearls with beads [the mother-of-pearl shell nucleus] has so far never been requested at this lab. Should we have such a request, we would be happy to comply. It would be an easy task to measure since we know the actual pearl diameter and therefore can calculate the magnification factor of the shadow on the fine grained film. [Here Hanni is referring to the shadow indicating the nacreous layer covering the nucleus, as seen in an x-ray.] Since generally accepted quality norms regarding nacre thickness do not exist, we could not use terms like 'very thick' or

K. Scarrett

Freshwater pearls in various shapes and hues.

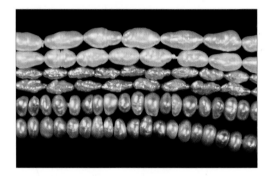

Whimsical Australian South Sea *baroque* cultured pearl in "Rabbit Pin" by Henry Dunay.

An exceptionally fine *Akoya* cultured pearl exhibiting the prized iridescent effect known as *orient.*

A. Muller; Golay Buchel

South Sea cultured pearls in white, black, golden.

Pacific Coast Pearls

Natural abalone pearls.

© Bill Kalina

Cultured abalone *mabé* pearls from New Zealand.

Magnificent *South Sea keshi* pearl necklace created by Asprey, London & New York.

Inset: Magnificent *conch* pearl in Edwardian necklace sold at auction (Antiquorum Fine Auctioneers, Geneva, Switzerland).

A range of *shapes, colors, sizes, luster* and *orient*. Note the pronounced orient in the small, white, irregularly shaped baroque, and note the difference in the color of each "white" pearl. As you compare the black pearls, note that while all are lovely, the largest black pearl is exceptionally large, but the shape is not as perfect as the smallest pearl, nor is the surface as smooth, nor luster as intense. Also note the subtle differences in the overtones seen in the black. The "black" pearl on the right has a hint of *blue*, the black baroque has a hint of *pink*, and the largest have a hint of *green*.

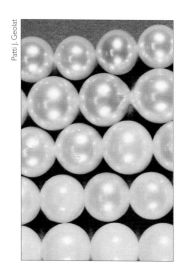

Patti J. Geolat

Broome Pearls

Note the range in *luster* and *orient*. The smaller, top strand exhibits very fine luster *and* orient; the bottom strand is typical of very poor quality, thin-nacre pearls that have no value or longevity.

Fine *"round white"* cultured pearls occur in a wide range of color from silver-white to cream white as you can see here; note differences in degree of "roundness." This is typical of South Sea cultured pearls because of their exceptionally thick nacre coating, and is to be expected in strands.

Freshwater Cultured Pearls from America

An assortment of American freshwater cultured pearls, including sticks, coins, ovals, bars, domés®, and distinctive jewelry creations.

© Kampsula

© K. Somos

Pearls from China

Chinese freshwater cultured pearls in a rainbow of colors and shapes.

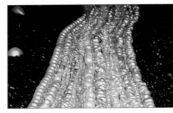

Left: Chinese freshwater pearl ring using range of hues.

© P. Crevoshay

K. Scarratt

© Trio

Pearls from Japan

Fine Akoya cultured pearl strands and earrings.

Exceptionally fine round Akoya cultured pearl necklace, earrings, and ring.

Lake Biwa freshwater, cultured baroque "stick" and "cross" pearls.

© Mikimoto

© Eve J. Alfillé, Ltd.

Pearls from Australia

A. Muller, Golay Buchel

Exceptionally fine round, silver-white Australian South Sea cultured pearl necklace and earrings, highlighting symmetrical pear-shape cultured pearl drops; round cultured pearl in ring; and large, distinctive baroque necklace.

A. Muller, Golay Buchel

Beautiful Tahitian natural *black* cultured pearls; an important strand (above) or a more casual necklace (below right). Elegant gentleman's dress set (below left).

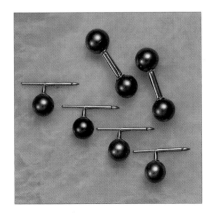

Pearls from Indonesia & the Philippines

South Sea cultured pearls in fancy *golden* colors and *"champagne"* cream tones.

Pearls from the Cook Islands

Flower brooch, or octopus, round, drop, or circlé, these pearls are striking. The rose overtone creates an *aubergine* color.

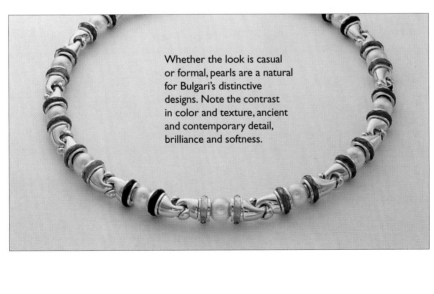

Whether the look is casual or formal, pearls are a natural for Bulgari's distinctive designs. Note the contrast in color and texture, ancient and contemporary detail, brilliance and softness.

From Hemmerle

Incredible "spider" brooch holding a huge brown conch pearl, the largest ever found.

From Trio

Whimsical creations
with baroque cultured
pearls are imaginative,
distinctive, and always
popular and wearable.

Dramatic elegance is created by Mauboussin using color. Above, triangular *cabochon* amethysts, *faceted* rubies, and diamonds with the softly sensual oval South Sea cultured pearls.

Yellow sapphire, diamonds, and Akoya cultured pearls in an elegant cuff bracelet.

Yellow sapphires, diamonds, and black cultured pearl drops.

From Mikimoto

One of the first cultured pearl pieces created by Mikimoto, this Edwardian period necklace dates from the early 1900s. Mikimoto is well known today for its contemporary classics (see ensemble in lower left grouping of "Pearls from Japan").

From Verdura

Exquisite brooch combines Renaissance feel with a playful, whimsical style — for which baroque cultured South Sea pearls are perfect.

Magnificent pear-shape Australian South Sea cultured pearls beautifully matched and gracefully graduated in a classic Van Cleef & Arpels design.

From Winston

Natural black Tahitian cultured pearls made their
world debut at Winston in 1978 and continue to be
sought by clients around the world.

Above: Natural pearl necklace of 32 pearls of 10.2-15.2 mm sold for $374,000 at Christie's.

Inset: The Sara, a gray natural pearl, fetched $470,600 (for a *single pearl*).

Left: La Régente, a *natural* pearl, skyrocketed at Christie's, to bring a record $859,000 for a *single pearl*.

Sotheby's

Australian South Sea cultured pearl necklace of record-breaking size — 16.0-20.1 mm — set a record price for pearls: $2,310,000 at Sotheby's.

Magnificent natural pearl and diamond tiara (1853), from the Thurn und Taxis treasury, brought approximately $650,000 at Sotheby's.

Extremely rare natural *green* color cultured South Sea pearl necklace with silver-gray overtones brought $160,000 at Sotheby's.

'thin' in a written report, but we could provide the actual nacre thickness in millimeters.

"For natural pearls:

- "The most important factors for selecting *natural* pearls in my opinion are: size, luster, shape, color, and orient. Do not expect the same uniformity that you are used to from beaded cultured pearls.

- "Check natural pearls to make sure there are not a lot of 'peeling areas' [Don't confuse this with the peeling of the nacre in a cultured pearl which will reveal the bead inside, indicating you will soon have no pearl at all. In natural pearls, there can be some surface peeling, especially if there are calcareous blemishes on or just beneath the surface. If you can find an expert who knows how, it might benefit the pearl to have it professionally "peeled" depending upon whether or not more serious blemishes might have formed underneath.].

- "Check natural pearls at the drill hole openings to be sure there is not much erosion.

- "When buying a natural pearl necklace, pay attention to the matching among the pearls in respect to color and graduation in size.

"For cultured pearls:

- "The most important factors for selecting *cultured* pearls in my opinion are: size, shape, nacre thickness, color, luster and orient.

- "Ask for color *authenticity* when pearls are any color other than white.

- "Correct any salesperson who speaks of 'Tahitian pearls' or 'South Sea pearls' without mentioning the word *cultured*! They are cultured, and this should always be indicated to avoid confusion.

- "For cultured pearls, go to a shop which specializes in cultured pearls and ask for them to explain what you need to know. Take the time to read a good book about pearls first, then compare the content with what the seller tells you; if there is not much difference in the information, then you can probably feel comfortable buying from this person."

George Kailis
Broome Pearls Pty Ltd. (Australia)

George Kailis is the Chairman of the M.G. Kailis Group of Companies, of which Broome Pearls is a part. He has been involved in the pearling industry for many years and has been part of making it what it has become today.

For Kailis the Best Moment Was the First

"The most exciting pearl to me was the first round pearl cultivated on our farm in Broome. I could see it glistening through the transparent membrane of the oyster, and knowing it to be a magnificent creation of nature, took immense pride in knowing, too, that we had contributed to its creation. The feeling of actually having had a hand in creating this beautiful pearl struck me in a poignant way and, to this day, I recall that moment as clearly as if it were yesterday."

Kailis Offers Solid Advice on Buying South Sea Pearls

"You should buy only from a reliable firm that specializes in pearls.

"A pearl is something very personal. When you look upon a pearl, if you immediately like it, if you feel something special, then you should buy it. If you don't have a personal feeling for the pearl, then don't buy it.

"Buy good quality. Although a low quality South Sea pearl may last forever because of its thick nacre coating, a pearl that has fine quality will be much more beautiful. And a beautiful pearl will be a constant source of pride as you wear it, and for your future generations as well.

"Look at pearls in *candlelight*. This is a good test; fine quality pearls will glow in the soft candlelight, while poor quality pearls will not.

"When choosing, keep personal preferences and lifestyle in mind. South Sea pearls come in many colors including white, pink-white, silver, blue, gold, and paler tints such as champagne, cognac, peach, French cream, yellow, and even pink. If the pearls are beautiful and lustrous, then choose whatever color most appeals to *you*.

"South Sea pearls come in many beautiful shapes. The rarest and most expensive are symmetrical shapes — round, teardrop, button. But again, if beautiful and lustrous, choose the shape that most appeals to you, and *best fits your lifestyle* (symmetrical shapes are considered more formal; baroque, semi-baroque and circle shapes, more casual)."

John Latendresse and Gina Latendresse American Pearl Company
(United States)

John Latendresse, Founder and Chairman of American Pearl Company, has almost 50 years' experience in the shell and pearling industry. The major supplier of shell required for cultured pearl production around the world, and always fascinated with the natural pearls of Tennessee and American waters, he is one of the premier experts on natural and cultured pearls alike. The innovator of techniques that have resulted in the production of the distinctive "American" freshwater cultured pearl (see Chapter 4), he has been referred to in recent years as the "father of the American cultured pearl." Gina Latendresse, President of American Pearl Company, is the daughter of John Latendresse and has 20 years' experience in the pearling industry working closely with her father and is also a Graduate Gemologist from the Gemological Institute of America.

John Latendresse Reminisces about a "Pearl Among Pearls"

"I still own the most exciting pearl I've ever seen because I could not bear to part with it. A natural pearl from the Black River in Arkansas, this magnificent pearl is larger than a dime, with a rich lustrousness, creamy white color, shimmering orient with a soft pink overtone, and a shape that is perfectly round! At 17.4 millimeters, we know of no other perfectly round natural pearl of such fine quality.

"I acquired this pearl in the 1950s. My shell buyer called to tell me that the diver who had found it wanted $500 for it. Based on the description over the phone, I authorized him to buy it immediately.

"When I actually saw this gem, I knew its worth far exceeded what I had paid. I felt that the diver, a transient itinerant who was not a young man, should have been paid much more than what I'd given for it, and I went personally in search of him to give him another $4,500. It took months to find out where he was — I learned he had died shortly before, and lay in a pauper's cemetery in Newport, Arkansas. I've always wished I could have found him sooner so he could have had a brief moment of feeling 'rich.' I often think of him, but not with sadness. For after all, how many can say at the end of a lifetime that they have realized their dream. His dream and that of every diver — discovering a marvelous treasure — came true."

Buying Tips from John and Gina Latendresse

"*Of all the factors that go into judging the quality of the pearl, the most important — and rarest — is orient.* A pearl with this characteristic is not only the most beautiful, it is your guarantee of fine quality and *natural* beauty. You can polish a pearl's surface and get a surface lustrousness; but 'orient' can't be artificially created on the surface of a pearl. Orient is something that comes from within, and it is what gives a fine pearl its true beauty.

"*When buying a strand, make sure the drill holes are all centered.* If they are not, the strand will not hang beautifully (this will really show up in shorter necklaces). To check for centered drilling, take one end of the strand and hold it up close to the eye, while holding the rest of the strand stretched out taut in front of you with the other hand. Now gaze down the strand. Looking at them this way, you'll easily spot off-center drilling.

"*Buy only from a fine jeweler who is knowledgeable about pearls and has a wide choice, in good quality.* Many jewelers now carry only three qualities: poor, medium, good. Few carry truly fine quality pearls because they are very expensive and many customers don't understand that lower prices usually mean inferior quality. Buying from a fine jeweler who carries only fine quality pearls means that your selection will have lasting beauty. If you buy medium or poor quality pearls, they will never become an heirloom...by the time mother hands them down to daughter, there won't be much nacre, and granddaughter will never see them!"

Richard Liddicoat
Gemological Institute of America
(United States)

Richard Liddicoat is Chairman of the Gemological Institute of America (GIA). Established in 1931, GIA is a respected education organization for jewelry professionals, and its Gem Trade Laboratory provides testing and quality reports on gemstones as well as on pearls.

Liddicoat on the Development — and Importance — of Lab Verification

"GIA began testing pearls to determine their origin — cultured or natural — in 1949 when the Institute took over the pearl testing equipment of what was then known as the Gem Trade Lab (GTL). Prior to that time, a few major firms had attempted in-house pearl testing, mainly with the endoscope — a time-consuming and now outdated instrument allowing only one pearl at a time to be tested.

"In the nearly 50 years of identifying pearls, GIA GTL has tested countless thousands of pearls, determining not only whether *cultured* or *natural* — but also if the color present was *natural* or *treated*. Throughout this time, the Laboratory has encountered, documented and developed testing methods for a number of new developments. In the early 1960s, tissue nucleated cultured pearls appeared on the market — causing an identification challenge, since this product was nucleated without a bead. The presence of the bead had been the telltale identifier of cultured pearls until that time."

Liddicoat on Determining Natural Color

"Shortly after these tissue nucleated cultured pearls were introduced, new colors came to market that were mainly the result of dyeing and in some cases irradiation. This resulted in testing more of this product, in many cases with the primary interest in natural or treated color, for which distinguishing criteria were developed by Robert Crowningshield. In 1961 GIA's interest in the origin of color of black and other fancy colored pearls led to published spectral criteria for identification of black pearls. This became important since later in the decade natural color black cultured pearls were nucleated in the French Polynesian atolls. The origin of color of such pearls became quite important, since the lookalike silver-salts treated colors were valued much lower than the natural color pearls.

"In addition to traditional natural and cultured pearls, the Laboratories routinely examine and report on unusual nacreless 'pearls' such as those from the conch shell and the very rare Bailer pearls."

Devin Macnow
Cultured Pearl Information Center
(United States)

Devin Macnow, executive director of the Cultured Pearl Information Center, heads a marketing and public relations team directly responsible for generating public awareness and developing marketing strategies for cultured pearls in the U.S. Communicating with fashion and lifestyle editors from over 10,000 publications and media outlets across the country, Macnow serves as an official spokesman for the Japanese and U.S. cultured pearl industry involving all aspects of cultured pearls from cultivation and history to marketing and promotions.

Macnow on the Value of a
Fine Japanese Akoya Cultured Pearl

"There are few events more amazing than the birth of a fine quality Akoya cultured pearl. The symbiotic relationship between man and oyster working together to form a true gem of rare beauty and value is indeed a labor of love and hard work. Though you may not realize it, it takes over 640,000 man/oyster hours of painstaking work to grow enough pearls so evenly matched in terms of lustre, size and color that they can be assembled into just one 16 inch necklace."

Macnow on the Versatility of a Cultured Pearl Necklace

"There are few items of jewelry a woman can own that are as versatile and will get as much use as a cultured pearl necklace. Pearls go with everything in a woman's wardrobe without ever feeling out of place. Unlike gold or diamond designs which may be bold and glitzy, cultured pearls have a soft, understated elegance that never fights for attention. Though clothing trends may change, pearls never go out of style. A simple strand of pearls is equally suitable for a business suit, a fancy cocktail dress, or jeans and a t-shirt."

Macnow on What to Look for When Buying Japanese Cultured Pearls

"Lustre by far is the most important quality aspect to look for when shopping for pearls. A cultured pearl with a high lustre is usually indicative of an exceptional quality pearl that will retain its beauty and value for generations to come. In addition, a bright and healthy lustre can often mask other minor surface imperfections such as bumps or pits."

Nicholas Paspaley
Paspaley Pearling Company (Australia)

Nicholas Paspaley is Chairman of Paspaley Pearling Company, founded by his father in 1935. Today it is the world's largest South Sea pearling company. Paspaley has been "immersed" in pearling his entire life, over 45 years.

Paspaley — Tales and Legends, and the Stuff of Dreams

"My father came from Greece with his family to the pearl coast of Australia — the Indian Ocean coast — in 1919. At this time there were only a handful of Europeans, the vast majority being primitive Aboriginal and Asian people, everyone living without running water, electricity, shops, government services, or any amenities. It was harsh, but the pearling life required sturdy stock; pioneers who were daring and bold. It still does.

"The allure of the rare and precious natural pearl that might be discovered within the oyster shell found here was a driving force for many — for they were considered the world's rarest and most beautiful pearls — but the pearling industry itself consisted of diving for the shell itself, for the mother-of-pearl shell lining that was needed to meet the world demand for *buttons*; Australian shell was the best quality and was used for 75% of the world's buttons. Natural pearls were sometimes discovered when the shells were open, but most were of low quality and not very valuable; a valuable pearl was a rare bonus.

"One night in 1935 whilst my father and his Asian and Aboriginal crew were aboard his lugger (a special type of fishing vessel), my father had a disturbing dream; he dreamed he had found a marvelous pearl, but was *murdered* by the crew. This was a common occurrence in those days for it was a lawless coast, and many awaited the death of a 'diver' — a highly coveted position — so that they might have the opportunity to become one. In any event, my father could not sleep. He went above deck for a cigarette and was further disturbed by a peculiar feel in the weather; although he could not tell for sure what it was that disturbed him, he always maintained that he could *feel* something different.

"The crew awoke as usual about an hour before sunrise, to ready things so the divers could be on the sea bed just as the sun rose above the shoreline. My father noted that they, too, felt uneasy about the weather. After the first drift (the lugger would drift with the tide along the pearl patch, dragging the divers about two miles across the ocean bed) the divers surfaced with the first catch of pearl shells — a very poor catch — complaining that a strange surge of water just above the bottom was washing them from side to side and stirring up mud and creating very poor visibility. My father knew this was a good shell bed (one could search for months to find a good one) and the skies were clear; only bad skippers left a good shell bed in fine weather (and it was not uncommon for skippers who wanted to leave under such circumstances to 'disappear' at sea.) Nonetheless, the bad feeling from his dream lingered, and he couldn't ignore the 'strange' unsettling feelings he had about the weather. He ordered his crew to prepare the lugger to move to another area, on the basis of poor visibility. And, still thinking of his dream, he advised them that he would open the catch of shells as the lugger made ready to get underway.

"He began to open the huge shells with his long-bladed knife. He opened the first shell, and there it was — the pearl in his dream!

"The blood rushed to his head and he felt goose bumps cover his entire body. Immediately thinking of his 'murder' in the dream, he slipped the pearl into his glove and hoped no one else had seen it. Fearing that he might be harmed, and using his uneasy feeling about the weather as an excuse, he immediately changed his orders to the crew and had them change course. He had them head for the nearest safe landfall, a river 24 hours away (they were 2-3 days away from their home port). There was a small aboriginal settlement a few miles up the river. When they arrived at the mouth of the river, it was sunset and the tide was low. Not wanting to remain on the lugger with the pearl, he rowed a small dinghy the several miles to the settlement, alone, leaving the lugger with his head diver, along with instructions to bring it to the settlement at high tide.

"Upon arriving at the settlement himself, my father arranged to travel immediately to his home port of Broome via truck. After several days travel through very unusual weather for that time of year — heavy rain and high wind — they arrived to learn that a terrible, severe cyclone had struck the pearling coast without warning. The 450 luggers out that day had no time to reach shelter. Most had been destroyed or damaged, and hundreds of crews drowned in the storm!

"Had my father not left when he did, his boat would surely have been lost at sea, as would the crew.

"This experience changed my father's life forever; he never ignored his instinct again. And as for the pearl, it was the finest he ever discovered in a life-long career as a 'master pearler' and helped propel him on his way to becoming one of the world's best known pearling 'greats.'

"I have also had my own experiences with life-threatening cyclones, sharks, crocodiles, not to mention the wild men! And there have been tragedies. But in my time the most memorable events have been the realisation of what was only a dream for my father — the development of the *cultivated South Sea pearl*, and a new and exciting pearling industry in Australia. This was a reality that had just begun to unfold for my father and his generation; one which I have seen, and helped, come to fruition."

On Australian South Sea Cultivated Pearls

"We believed that the wild pearl oyster species found in Australia — that which as I mentioned earlier was known to produce the most beautiful *natural* pearls — could produce *cultured* pearls as well. We also believed that if we could succeed, our pearls would look more like real pearls because of their exceptionally thick nacre coating.

"The invention of plastic buttons in the 1950s resulted in the decimation of our fleets; demand for mother-of-pearl virtually disappeared. This turn of events provided the major catalyst for the Australian industry to intensify efforts to successfully produce cultivated pearls; it was our only hope for economic survival. Research and development began, but fine South Sea cultivated pearls have only been a commercial reality for the last 15 years.

"During my father's pioneering days on his pearl 'farm,' one of Australia's first, it was generally accepted that the ultimate success would be to produce a perfect, round, 15 millimeter pearl — this had been achieved only once or twice in the first ten years of this new 'farming' industry. As I gained experience, I began to have a dream of my own, to do the impossible — to make pearl *strands* consisting entirely of pearls over 15 millimeters.

"The production of cultivated pearls from these pearl producing oysters (commonly, but incorrectly, called 'South Sea pearls,' a term now used to refer to the large pearls produced anywhere in the world by these oysters) was a special challenge, as it still is, because *wild oysters are used, in their natural habitat.* As a result, methods had to be developed that differed radically from those developed by the Japanese, requiring more time, higher risks. We had many failures, but after many years of research and development of new techniques, working with the Hamaguchi family we finally succeeded in producing a perfect pearl of 20 millimeters! — the most beautiful pearl I could ever have imagined.

"Today, South Sea production is still limited by comparison to world-wide production, but the size, quality, and beauty have surpassed even the wildest imaginings of our forefathers."

Kenneth Scarratt
Asian Institute of Gemological Sciences
(AIGS) (Thailand)

Kenneth Scarratt is Director of Laboratory Services, Education and Research at the Asian Institute of Gemological Sciences. He has been conducting research on pearls, and evaluating natural and cultured pearls from every part of the world, for over 22 years. Much of his work on pearls was carried out during his 18 years with the Gemmological Association and Gem Testing Laboratory of Great Britain, of which he was Chief Executive and Director of Laboratory Services. Since assuming the Directorship of the laboratory at the AIGS, he has been instrumental in establishing new procedures and standards for pearl evaluation. AIGS is the only international laboratory which, at this time, indicates the thickness of the nacre coating — in actual millimeters — on pearl grading reports.

Scarratt Gets at the Core of
What's Important in Selecting Fine Pearls

"Put very simply, we regard nacre thickness in cultured pearls — that is, the actual depth of the pearly coating over the mother-of-pearl shell bead — as the most important factor in selecting pearls. After all, if the nacre on a cultured pearl is so thin that it disappears after six months, all the purchaser is going to be left with is a row of shell beads. We believe that knowing the actual nacre thickness on pearls is necessary information — in fact, essential — for an individual to make a rational judgment when buying or selling cultured pearls. This is why we consider the examination of nacre thickness, *and its inclusion on our pearl reports,* so important. Many in the pearling industry do not want this information provided. Furthermore, for most laboratories the very high cost of the sophisticated, advanced radiography equipment necessary to obtain this information, even on undrilled pearls, is a deterrent. Nonetheless, we hope that other major laboratories will follow our lead in the near future.

"At this time we do not provide *grading* on pearl *quality*. However, we continue to investigate all possibilities and as the situation develops over the next few years with regard to establishing a universally recognized pearl grading system, it may be that further information of a 'grading nature' might be incorporated."

Maurice Shire
Maurice Shire, Inc. (United States)

Maurice Shire is President of Maurice Shire, Inc., a firm specializing today in importing colored gemstones. He began his 50-year career in this field as a jewelry apprentice in Paris, at the age of twelve. His earliest experiences centered around natural pearls, and few can match his eyes for these precious treasures, or his skill at pearl "peeling."

Shire on Recognizing Natural Pearls When You See Them

"I have worked with many great people over the years, but two giants in the natural pearl world are really responsible for my love, appreciation, and 'eye' for these wonders.

"Almost 50 years ago while I was working in a very fine jewelry store as an assistant buyer, the company purchased an important jewelry estate through a bank. The estate cost close to a quarter million dollars, which was a lot of money at the time. We had to go through the estate and list each piece separately for inventory purposes, indicating its value. When it came to the fine diamonds, emerald, ruby and sapphire pieces in the estate, we had no problem estimating value; but when it came to a cultured pearl necklace that was part of it, we had no idea (at that time, most of the pearls sold by fine jewelers were natural pearls). Since we had to put a value on them, and to be fair to our customers, we contacted several cultured pearl dealers and the general consensus was that its fair retail value was about $950. And so it was tagged.

"The necklace was composed of 55 cream-rose colored pearls, all perfectly spherical, highly lustrous, and without any blemishes on their surfaces; the strand graduated from 9.5 millimeters at the center down to 7 millimeters at each end. The necklace remained in the safe until one day, when a beautiful lady entered the store about eighteen months later asking for a cultured pearl necklace. We showed her the only one we had, the one in the safe, which she liked very much. However, she wanted us to add a larger pearl — one that measured 10.5 millimeters — for the center pearl, and another measuring 9.5 to add to what had originally been the large center pearl, so that there would be two 9.5 millimeter pearls to flank the new center pearl. I gave her an estimate on what it would cost, about $400 more (at that time, in a graduated necklace the center pearl represented about ⅓ the total cost of the necklace). She authorized me to proceed, but would not even give me a deposit, telling me she would pay nothing until the necklace was complete and met her expectations, but that if she liked it, she would pay for it right then and there. We agreed, and I, of course, proceeded to have the necklace completed as quickly as possible.

"I immediately went with the necklace to visit an old gentleman named Leonard Rosenthal, who was at that time the 'Roi de la Perle' — the 'Pearl King' (he was the largest dealer of natural pearls in the world). After explaining the purpose of my visit, Mr. Rosenthal picked up the strand by the clasp with his left hand, letting the remainder rest in the palm of his right hand. He leaned back in his chair, looked at the necklace, and in less time than it takes to say 'Jack Robinson,' he exclaimed, 'Maurice, you *are* aware that there are natural pearls in this strand, aren't you'!

"Of course I was not, nor were any of the many people who had handled the necklace before me. He then proceeded to take out a pearl chart and number each pearl, and then mark each that was natural — 23 out of 55, he told me, were natural. I went to the laboratory of the Gemological Institute of America to get an x-ray and verify this. The GIA stuck a little piece of black tape on each pearl that the x-ray showed to be natural (which they still do today); 23 were natural. They were, of course, the same 23 that Mr. Rosenthal had spotted with his 75-year-old eyes.

"Back in Mr. Rosenthal's office I was, as one can imagine, very excited at this adventure and very impressed with the old man's wisdom and knowledge. We removed the natural pearls and replaced them with cultured pearls, completing the cultured pearl necklace that the lovely lady had requested. But for three days prior to her coming to get them, I studied the cultured pearls in comparison to the natural pearls we had removed. I was determined to discover the differences that Mr. Rosenthal saw at a glance. But to no avail. Finally, I put both strands in my pocket and returned to Mr. Rosenthal where the following dialogue ensued:

"'Mr. Rosenthal, I have spent the last three days trying to see the differences between these two strands and I just can't. I am young and ambitious, and yearn to learn as much as possible about gems. I also realize that there are professional secrets that one imparts only to one's children or grandchildren. But might you share your secret with me and tell me how you were able to spot the 23 natural pearls so quickly, with just your eyes?'

"Mr. Rosenthal replied, 'My dear Maurice, when you will have handled pearls for 45 years, you too will be able to see the difference immediately.'

"Of course I was not happy with his reply and thought the old fox simply didn't wish to share the secret; I felt very frustrated with his answer. Meanwhile, Mr. Rosenthal bought the natural pearls, which had a retail value at that time of about $6,000 — over six times what we'd paid for the entire necklace of 55 pearls.

"Independent by nature, and anxious to try to fly on my own, I left the retail end of our trade and became a wholesale broker. About a year later, Mr. René Bloch, another older and prominent natural pearl dealer, offered to teach me the natural pearl business so that I might over a period of time buy out his inventory so he could retire. About an hour after he began to instruct me in the 'art' of valuing natural pearls through comparing pearls in his own inventory, I could no longer contain myself; I related what Mr. Rosenthal had told me. 'If you are teaching me the technicalities, and I am to buy your business one day, start by sharing the secret of how one tells natural from cultured pearls.' Mr. Bloch smiled and said, 'Mr. Rosenthal told you the truth; one day you will see it without even realizing it.' About two years later a jeweler walked into our office with five pearl necklaces one of his wealthy and prominent customers wanted to sell and he hoped we would make him an offer. I quickly glanced at them one by one, just to get a quick general idea of what he had, and as I looked upon the third necklace I found myself saying, 'This one is cultured.' At that moment I remembered the words of Mr. Rosenthal and I almost said, 'Eureka...I've made it!'"

Robert Wan
Tahiti Pearls (Tahiti, French Polynesia)

Robert Wan is the Chairman of Tahiti Pearls and a legendary pioneer in the Tahitian black pearl industry. Over the past twenty years he has revolutionized the industry and brought naturally black Tahitian cultured pearls to the world of connoisseurs.

A Little-Known Fact from Days of Old

"At the peak of the mother-of-pearl button industry (in the 1920s and 30s) the phenomenal feats of Polynesian divers became legendary. Some divers, weighted down with lead, plunged deeper than 40 meters with just the oxygen in their lungs. A pair of glasses, gloves, and a net comprised their only equipment. With this and nothing more they risked encounters with sharks and moray eels, as well as the deadly 'bends,' in order to harvest the shells that had become the prime export of the atolls (this exotic, dark 'mother-of-pearl' was in great demand for decorative inlay and dark buttons). But there was always the dream, for most an elusive dream, that drew them back into the sea — that one day, one of the shells they brought to the surface might reveal a rare, magnificent, and valuable black pearl."

Polynesia, Land of the Deep and Mysterious, Creates a True Romantic — Wan on Why He Likes Pearls

"The woman and the pearl, I love them both — and the one and the other seem inseparable. They have so many traits in common: mystery, allure, smoothness and sensuality. Each enhances the other's natural beauty.

"Like a woman, a pearl needs care; it is something precious, not to be taken for granted. Just as it needs special care and attention to keep its lustrousness, so a woman only shines from within when she receives special care and attention.

"And when selecting a pearl — like a woman — never compromise on *quality*. It is the key to having a lasting future together!"

Torio Yamamoto
Yamakatsu Pearl Company (Japan)

Yamakatsu was founded in 1931 and over its 65 year history has gained worldwide respect for cultivation, processing, and distribution of high quality pearls. Torio Yamamoto is Managing Director of Yamakatsu and has been involved in all aspects of the industry for the past 40 years. Here he shares some of his thoughts on what is important when selecting pearls.

From Yamamoto, Pearls of Wisdom on Selecting Your Pearls

"The first thing you must ask yourself is whether or not you think the pearl is beautiful. A fine pearl is one that everyone will agree is beautiful. After looking at pearls for a while, you will know what a beautiful pearl looks like; it is something on which there is universal agreement. If it is beautiful to behold, it is a fine pearl; if it is not beautiful, it is not a fine pearl.

"When buying pearls it is especially important to choose a fine jeweler, with a good reputation, who *specializes* in pearls. This way you will be able to see a wider selection and have differences properly explained. If you just go into a store and buy just any pearls you happen to see, you may be very unhappy later. You should go to several fine jewelers and compare what you see and listen to what the jewelers have to say about their pearls. This will help you learn to see differences and understand them; it will also give you greater confidence and appreciation for the pearls you ultimately select.

"Personally, I recommend pearls with good color and rich luster — even if it means getting a less perfect shape or having some small spots on the surface.

"Avoid pearls which have blemishes that are so pronounced you can feel them easily with your nails, or on which your nails actually get caught."

Benjamin Zucker
Precious Stones Company (United States)

Benjamin Zucker is President of Precious Stones Company, a firm specializing in very fine colored gemstones and pearls. He is a gem supplier, lecturer and author, and serious collector (as was his father before him); The Walters Museum in Baltimore, Maryland, houses part of the Zucker Collection of exceptional antique jewelry and gems. Pearls have always been of special interest, and he has devoted a beautiful chapter to them in his book, Gems & Jewels: A Connoisseur's Guide.

Zucker Knows a Trick or Two When Selecting Pearls

"Luster is the single most important factor when selecting pearls. To judge it, don't look straight down on them or examine them at too close a range. Look at them at a distance — the same distance at which you'd view yourself in a mirror. Now ask yourself: do the pearls have luster or not? Follow your first instinct.

"Shape is very important. In round pearls, the shape should be as round as possible. If the luster is good, and the pearls are round, however, they will be expensive. If you can't afford very round pearls with high luster, consider pearls slightly less round before you settle for pearls with reduced lustrousness.

"Cleanliness is something we weight at 30%; luster at 70%."

Pearls, History, and Art

"I love antique jewels, especially those containing pearls. I also love the connection between pearls and the sea, and jewelry in which this connection is embodied.

"Pay attention to the great artists and you will notice a special attraction between the great masters and pearls. Perhaps the pearl speaks to the soul of the artist, to the sensual and creative side. Perhaps it is because of the timelessness of the pearl, and the artist's own subconscious yearning to be captured in time."

Chapter 11

Great Jewelers on Great Pearls

Pearls have always been a favorite of great jewelers, inspiring magnificent creations throughout history. From the glorious pearl jewels of the Renaissance Age to the present, pearls have stimulated the imagination and challenged the jeweler to find the perfect setting.

The modern "cultured pearl" brought with it a fresh opportunity; for the first time ever, jewelers could depend upon *quantities* of pearls and reproduce designs in ways never before possible with natural pearls because of their limited supply.

We have asked some of the world's leading jewelers to provide us with some of their own thoughts on pearls, and to show us pieces they personally consider to be exceptional. In these pages and in the color insert section you will see some wonderful pearl jewelry, and gain a greater understanding of what we mean when we say that there truly is a pearl for every personal style and every special occasion!

Boucheron

Boucheron is one of the great French jewelry houses. Founded in 1858, it was the firm of Boucheron that introduced the use of diamond rondelles with pearls to create a distinctive yet classic look that is very much in vogue even to this day.

Alain Boucheron, President of Boucheron, on Pearls

"The most expensive gem I've ever had is a white pearl with a baroque shape; it weighed 8,000 grains (2,000 carats)!

"To appreciate a diamond, the surface must be pierced to release the dazzling display of color that can come from its heart; but to appreciate the pearl, the eye must simply gaze upon its surface to behold its soft color and peaceful beauty.

"One of the most wonderful pieces ever created by the house of Boucheron was a pearl necklace made in 1889 under the supervision of Frederic Boucheron. It was the first necklace ever to combine pearls and diamond 'rondelles,' an innovation in design that became an instant success that is occasionally seen even today, over 100 years later.

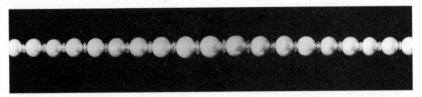

Portion of natural pearl necklace made by Frederic Boucheron in 1889, the first necklace ever to combine pearls with diamond "rondelles." An understated look — but very important — and one still in vogue today.

"The necklace contained 29 large natural pearls (953 grains) and 28 pierced diamond 'rondelles' [diamonds cut into a circular shape with a hollow center, resembling a wheel or doughnut]; the clasp contained a black pearl weighing 65 grains, encircled by diamonds.

"The necklace was designed by the legendary designer Paul LeGrand (who designed for Boucheron from 1863-1867 and from 1871-1892). It was LeGrand who conceived the idea of combining pearls with the 'new' diamond rondelle, an innovation of the great nineteenth-century diamond cutter Bordinckx (the first cutter in Western Europe to understand how to pierce the diamond and cut it in this unique way) who was closely linked to the house of Boucheron from 1880 until his death in 1892. LeGrand thought that the soft, subtle beauty of the pearl would be beautifully highlighted by contrast with the sparkle of these diamond 'separators' and create a distinctive and important — yet understated — jewel. History has proved him correct.

"This necklace reappeared on the market recently and was acquired in November 1995 for 550,000 French francs (approximately $100,000)."

Bulgari

Founded in Rome in the late 1800s, Bulgari is recognized today as one of the world's premiere jewelers, with salons in twenty countries worldwide. The design is fresh, bold, and distinctive, often characterized by its creative use of color, texture, and unusual combinations.

Nicola Bulgari on Pearls

"I love pearls for their softness and simplicity. No other gem is as simple, elegant, and *sensual.* Yes, I mean sensual — there is a softness and mystery to pearls, and like a woman, they can surprise you; you can find them — alluringly and charmingly — in places you might never expect. They can be demure and elegant, or whimsical and playful; they can *quietly* capture your attention, or *demand* to be noticed.

"I think pearls have become even more popular as people have become more fascinated by things that are organic. They have always been one of our favorite gems. We offer an unusually wide range of choices from the most simple to the sublime; here you will find romantic simplicity, unusual versatility or regal elegance, depending upon the occasion.

"Perhaps our Italian heritage and the influence of the magnificent Italian Renaissance jewels have had an influence on our design. As did our forefathers, we love color — we are perhaps best known for our innovative use of colored gems — and we love to intermingle colored gems with pearls in distinctive ways. We often intersperse the neutral tones of white and cream-colored pearls with colored gemstones to create interesting contrasts; the color is enhanced by contrast to the soft neutrality of the pearls, and the soft lustrousness of the pearl is enhanced by contrast to the color.

"We also love to use colored gemstones in *cabochon* cuts (a type of cut which has a smooth, rounded surface) rather than faceted gemstones with pearls because we think their rich, almost velvety character is a natural with the soft, rich character of the pearl. Together, they create a lushness unrivaled by any other.

"We often add the warmth of gold as well, alternating interlocking gold elements with colored gemstone rondelles [circular, doughnut-shaped elements used to separate beads, pearls, and so on] for an especially striking look that one can immediately identify as a 'Bulgari' look. You can see this in our simplest designs and in our most elaborate.

"When using pearls alone, we especially love golden pearls — I think they are especially sensual — and the Tahitian black pearls can be spectacular, and very dramatic. Americans are just beginning to appreciate the fancy colors, especially the yellow and golden tones, but I think they will become very much in demand.

"Whatever type of pearl one is considering, it must be of very good quality. Most of the pearls used in our jewelry are cultured since we cannot depend on an adequate supply of natural pearls; we reserve natural pearls for special, one-of-a-kind creations. But whether cultured or natural, fine quality is very important — poor quality pearls are not as lovely...nor will they last for future generations.

"We will always create wonderful pearl designs, because people love pearls; they always have and they always will. It's as simple as that."

Cartier

The house of Cartier was founded in Paris 150 years ago and opened its New York salon in 1908. Known around the world today, the name of Cartier is synonymous with great design and innovation, classic style, and fine quality.

Cartier Chairman Ralph Destino on Pearls

"Pearls have, historically, occupied a preeminent position here at Cartier. Our most dramatic, and perhaps most famous experience, involved a magnificent natural pearl necklace. Let me tell you about it:

"In 1915 Cartier made history by offering the first pearls to be priced over $1 million — $1.2 million to be exact! You can imagine what this would be in 1995 dollars. The necklace was placed on exhibition in Paris, then in London, and finally arrived in New York in the fall of 1916. All the great ladies of New York — the Astors, the Vanderbilts, and so on — rushed to admire them, but no one was prepared to pay the price that Cartier was asking.

"While the pearls were making the 'Grand Tour' in Europe, another seemingly unrelated event was taking place; Grace Vanderbilt, the Grand Dame of New York society, sold her mansion on the southwest corner of 52nd and Fifth Avenue and moved uptown to the 'country,' at Fifth Avenue and 85th Street. Her young neighbor across the street on the southeast corner of Fifth and 52nd, Maisie Plant, wanted to follow suit. After all, if the neighborhood was 'déclassé' for Grace Vanderbilt, it wasn't good enough for Maisie! So she

Maisie Plant, wearing her magnificent double strand natural pearl necklace for which she traded her Fifth Avenue mansion to Cartier!

decided to sell her mansion and move uptown as well. She put it on the market, coincidentally, for $1.2 million.

"We now return to the pearl necklace. When it made its debut at Cartier's New York salon — a small establishment on the second floor of a building at 54th and Fifth — all of New York society came to marvel at the pearls. None marvelled more than Maisie Plant. She wanted them. However, her husband, normally a most generous man, refused to consider such a price for pearls. Well, thought Maisie, the mansion is mine, and since I'm going to move uptown anyway (her husband being fully prepared to put his money into prime real estate) — she went to Cartier and proposed a swap...the mansion in exchange for the pearl necklace. And Louis Cartier accepted! The firm of Cartier has been situated in the former Plant mansion since that time, and this building has become a great New York landmark. Unfortunately for Maisie, she didn't anticipate the depression, war, and introduction of cultured pearls; her necklace was sold at auction in 1957 by Parke-Bernet (now Sotheby's) for a mere $170,000; the current value of the Fifth Avenue mansion I'll leave to your imagination.

"I love pearls, but there are pearls...and then there are *pearls*! One could say that the foundation of any woman's jewelry wardrobe would begin with the pearl. I myself made a small strand of pearls for a six-year-old girl — her first piece of jewelry (not to mention, *Cartier* jewelry). Pearls form the beginning of any jewelry collection; they can begin in childhood and then go on from there to the amazing rarities that exist.

"There are pearls that are truly treasures because of their rarity, and there are those that are *treasured* because of the sentiment. Both can be of huge significance, but each for a different reason. In that sense, pearls may be the most versatile of all of nature's gems.

"Pearls are meant to be touched and felt, and placed upon the skin; put them on and see how you feel in them before making any purchase decision.

"We offer our clientele only the finest quality pearls. In white pearls this means pearls that have high luster, are perfectly round with a rose color and clear skins, and well matched. We recommend that clients consider these factors first; while you must be comfortable with the size, we recommend that size should be the last consideration, with rare exceptions. When one can't afford a long pearl necklace in fine quality in the size they want, we suggest that they acquire a shorter necklace, and add to it over a period of time rather than sacrifice quality."

Hemmerle Juweliere

Founded in 1893 in Munich, Germany, Hemmerle Jewelers has established a reputation for exclusive design, extraordinary quality, and an especially sensitive use of color to create a particular mood or feeling in its jewelry creations.

Mr. Stefan Hemmerle, President, GEBR., Hemmerle, on Pearls

"When selecting pearls, the country of origin is important since each produces a slightly different pearl; we use cultured Akoya pearls from Japan, South Sea pearls from Australia or Burma, black pearls from Tahiti, and fancy yellow pearls from Indonesia.

"We enjoy working with natural pearls as well as cultured pearls. In natural pearls, a creamier color is acceptable, as are off-shapes; off-shapes can be very distinctive in their own way.

"In Japanese cultured pearls the first thing we look for is very high, very intense luster. If luster is intense, we will accept slight deficiencies in shape and surface perfection. We prefer sizes between 7-10 millimeters in diameter, in both graduated and non-graduated styles.

"We find Australian South Sea cultured pearls becoming increasingly popular. Many prefer the silver-white color, but we prefer a color somewhat more creamy, looking more like the natural pearls. We look for a rich luster and good matching in their shape. Graduated necklaces containing pearls ranging between 10-12 millimeters are especially desirable, but very difficult to find; necklaces containing pearls between 14-16 millimeters create a very important appearance.

"In fancy color pearls we especially like the 'black' pearls and intense yellow pearls. In the case of the Tahitian black type, although the rarest colors are midnight black we prefer those in medium to deep gray shades because we find them the most charming against the skin. Regarding the natural color yellow pearls, we find the most beautiful tints to be the intense yellows and deep gold; these pearls are wonderful curiosities and are enjoying tremendous interest on the world market.

"Speaking of curiosities, one of the most magnificent pieces of jewelry we have ever created contains a great pearl that is indeed a curiosity: *the largest conch pearl ever found.* It is the most interesting we have ever owned. A dark brown, football-shaped natural conch pearl from the giant 'horse conch,' it weighs over 111 carats and measures 27.47 millimeters in size. It was discovered by a Spanish expedition and given by the leader of this expedition to our firm, and we have just completed a magnificent 'spider' brooch with this pearl at its center. Since the value of this pearl cannot be easily estimated because it is indeed unique, we have placed a value of $100,000 on the pearl alone."

Krikorian

Krikor Krikorian, an American designer, was the first American ever to win the Grand Prix award in the International Pearl Design contest. Here he explains what he has created.

Krikor Krikorian on His Award-Winning Necklace

"I wanted to create a necklace that freely flowed around the neck of a woman, creating a light and natural feeling while giving the appearance of a clinging vine; the vine is composed of freshwater pearls that are held together by 18 karat yellow gold wiring with an inlay of diamonds.

"I've always enjoyed sculpting things out of the earth's natural resources....this is what inspired me to use pearls; besides their soft appearance and mysterious luster, cultured pearls are an organic gem. I like that."

International Pearl Design contest Grand Prix winner by Krikorian, showing dramatic use of freshwater "stick" pearls.

Mauboussin

Mauboussin, founded in 1827, is one of the oldest and most respected of the French jewelry salons; some of Mauboussin's creations can be found among the Crown jewels of Europe.

Patrick Mauboussin, Chairman of Mauboussin, on Pearls

"We love pearls and have created some spectacular pearl jewels for many illustrious personalities in our 169-year history. But one of the most fabulous creations we have ever produced is a recent one, designed around a magnificent black pearl from French Polynesia. A beautiful, gem-encrusted cup, this true 'objet d'art' was presented to Emperor Akhito and Empress Michiko of Japan on their official visit to Paris in 1994. Knowing of their

passion for the water, this whimsical 'objet d'art' highlighted a playful fish, precariously balanced on its lip and holding in its mouth this great pearl, this treasure from the deep. The most talented artisans, reflecting the finest of French workmanship, sculpted the cup from rock crystal and the fish from tourmaline, fashioning a perfect background against which to suspend the wonderful pearl."

Patrick Mauboussin with Empress Michiko

Bernard Janot, Gemological Expert and Director of Gem Buying for Mauboussin, on Pearls

"Much of the appeal of the pearl results from the fact that it comes from a living creature and is truly a natural product, not needing man's touch to transform it; even the great artisans can add nothing to its beauty.

"Pearls have a virgin brightness that sets them apart from other precious stones and gives them an allure that appeals to everyone.

"The incomparable radiance and sheen of the pearl — and the assurance of an adequate supply not possible with natural pearls — has created something of a renaissance among French jewelers. We love the amazing and charming palette of colors offered by pearls today, from white to dark gray and black, from pinky beige to bronze to gold, and with the subtle nuances created by overtones of green, black and pink, the range of shades is almost infinite. Worn against the naked skin, a lively and lustrous pearl reflects a thousand other shades, and like a magician, highlights the femininity of the woman who wears them. Can there be any doubt that the pearl has a special allure for anyone who is romantic? Perhaps this is why we French have a special regard for pearls."

Mikimoto

The firm of Mikimoto was established by, and celebrates, the man who developed and perfected the art of culturing pearls, Kokichi Mikimoto. This firm specializes in only the finest quality cultured pearls, and now has salons in Tokyo, London, Paris, New York, and San Francisco. In addition, Mikimoto pearls can be seen in many fine jewelry stores worldwide.

Kikuichiro Ishii,
President of Mikimoto America, on Pearls

"What we sell really tells you what we think is most important — *quality.* Our pearls represent the top 3%-5% of pearls harvested. They are selected for their *very thick* nacre, luster, color and shape. Nacre thickness is very important, maybe the most important. Of course, this means that pearls that rank exceptionally high in other factors such as surface perfection and shape will be even rarer and more costly, for the longer the pearl is in the oyster — to get thick nacre — the more that can go wrong.

"We do not stress size, but beauty. Look for *luster* above all, and select the best quality you can afford.

"Buy pearls only from a reliable store that will have a broad selection of good quality pearls; usually jewelers who have a good inventory of fine quality pearls have prices that are more reasonable for the fine quality than jewelers who carry a more limited stock."

Koichi Takahashi,
Senior Vice President, Mikimoto, on Pearls

"If you have a set budget, don't sacrifice quality; instead, consider these alternatives —

• A slightly smaller pearl — such as a strand of 7-7 ½ millimeter pearls rather than a strand of 7 ½-8. You may be surprised to find that a slightly smaller strand of very fine pearls will look as large as a larger strand of mediocre quality.

• Compromise on the *length of the strand* you want; get a shorter necklace, and *add to it* over a period of time.

• Look at 'convertible clasps' that can add versatility so you can get the most usage from a single necklace."

Tiffany & Co.

Tiffany & Co. is one of America's oldest and most prestigious jewelry firms. Established in 1837, the name Tiffany has become synonymous with quality, distinctive and innovative design, and rare and unusual gems. Today Tiffany has stores and boutiques across America and in major cities throughout Asia and Europe.

Jeanne B. Daniel, Senior Vice President, Tiffany & Co., on Pearls

"We encourage customers to shop with a critical eye. Several physical features must be evaluated: size, shape, color, luster, orient, surface, and matching. Ask yourself, 'Are the pearls well-matched? Are the surfaces free of obvious flaws? Do the color and luster appear to emanate from deep within the pearl?'

"Various environmental influences make high quality pearls increasingly rare. When purchasing pearl jewelry these conditions compel the wise shopper to seek out a well-respected jeweler experienced with the gem. Tiffany rejects far more pearls than it accepts, and the company's minimum standards for pearls rival the best quality available anywhere.

"Throughout its 158-year history, Tiffany & Co. has had a special romance with the pearl. In 1908, the most definitive work ever done on pearls — *The Book of the Pearl* — was written by George Kunz, America's foremost gemologist and Tiffany's vice president. His emphasis on acquiring pearls of exceptional quality and luster is still practiced by Tiffany.

"The Tiffany Pearl Collection has always been simple, classic, and elegant, as illustrated in the modern interpretation of an Edwardian period design shown here. This platinum and diamond corset is based on a late 19th century piece now housed in Tiffany's Permanent Collection. It is adorned with floret, lattice, tassel and bow motifs, supported by a four-strand cultured pearl choker (the original contains natural

pearls). The pearl strands can be replaced with a black velvet ribbon. Each of the corset motifs are interpreted in earrings, a pendant, and a pearl and diamond strand. This is truly a great pearl creation."

Trio

Trio Pearl Company is well known to the world traveler visiting Hong Kong. This 40-year-old firm specializes in the finest of pearls, and has developed an illustrious worldwide clientele.

Sammy Chow, Chairman of Trio, on Pearls

"I believe the most important thing to look for in pearls is the high luster and the smoothness of its coating. Luster is what gives pearls 'life' and richness, which could only be beautifully manifested if the skin is smooth. What renders pearl its luster is the thickness of its layers of coating. The color and shape are also equally important, as the rounder and the larger they are, the more valuable (assuming that they have the high luster and smooth coating that is most important). The most sought after color is white with a tinge of pink, but there is also great demand for black and gold. Personally, I feel that it is luster and color that attract attention before anything else.

"The most basic component of every jewelry collection should be a basic strand of Japanese cultured pearls. The most popular size ranges from 7 to 9 millimeters. South Sea pearls are highly prized, and the perfect choice for important gifts.

"The most important necklaces we ever sold were two South Sea pearl necklaces of the rarest 'gem quality' pearls ranging in size from 11-15 ½ millimeters. These were *triple strand* necklaces. The first was acquired by a European princess over a period of ten years; she first collected a matched strand of white pearls, then over the years, amassed another strand to match them, but in black! The finishing touch, however, was the third strand she collected to match the other two, in deep gold!

"The second necklace was a triple strand, *opera length* necklace — with one strand in white, one in black, and the third in gold! Necklaces like these are labors of love and passion...they take years to create, but when the task is done, they are truly something to behold."

Van Cleef & Arpels

The French jewelry firm of Van Cleef & Arpels has been recognized as a world leader since it was founded in 1906. With salons now in 32 cities and offices in the United States, Europe and the Far East, it is known for innovation in design, unusual production techniques such as *invisibly set* jewels, very fine workmanship, artistry, and whimsical, romantic motifs.

Henri Barguirdjian, President
of Van Cleef & Arpels, U.S.A., on Pearls

"Today most people don't know what pearls are. They think *cultured pearls* are *real** pearls. They don't know the difference and this is a shame. The finest quality cultured pearls are very lovely, desirable and expensive, but they cannot compare to the exquisite natural pearl. Natural pearls are truly rare and exotic and each is unique; cultured pearls are available in abundance.

"At Van Cleef & Arpels we use very fine cultured pearls for most of our classic pearl designs and real pearls for unique, one-of-a-kind jewels. We find there is still a market for real pearls, and each year we succeed in acquiring a considerable number for our most discerning clientele despite the fact that they are rare and difficult to obtain.

"The market is now flooded with large cultured pearls, but often they are not fine, and they are *not* rare in such quality. Most people believe they are buying something very different from what they are really buying. They don't understand how much of the pearl is the bead placed in the oyster by man. In some cases — where poor quality cultured pearls are concerned — their money would be better spent on fake pearls!

"Whether cultured or real, we stress quality. There is really nothing more to be said. We look partially for 'orient' [see Chapter 5] which, unfortunately, is not often seen now, as well as luster, shape, surface perfection. Size is not as important, in our opinion. In point of fact, a famous client recently came to us for a pair of very large drop pearls — the bigger the better. I showed her several pair, the smallest of which was far superior in quality. I had to fight at great length with the woman to convince her to pay more attention to the smaller pair; I even went so far as to tell her that if size was so important, she would be better advised to buy a pair of costume earrings where she could easily find a huge pair of drops! Gradually she began to see the difference in the pearls and understand and appreciate the quality in the 'smaller' — which were hardly small by normal standards — and she bought these.

"We struggle sometimes to help our clients see and appreciate the quality differences in pearls, but after all is said, whether cultured or real, it is fine *quality* that makes *wonderful* pearls! That's all there is to it."

* Mr. Barguirdjian uses the term "real" to denote *natural* pearls; the FTC requires that the term "real pearls" only be used in reference to natural.

Verdura

The firm of Verdura was the creation of the Duke of Verdura, Fulco Santostefano della Cerda. Born in Sicily in 1898, Verdura became one of Chanel's favorite costume jewelry designers, designing her most revolutionary creations. He opened his own firm in New York in 1939, in an upstairs suite on Fifth Avenue. An immediate success among a wealthy and avant garde clientele, Verdura combined a Renaissance character with his whimsical style; his creations were classic and wearable, yet witty and unconventional. And so Verdura remains today.

Edward Landrigan, President of Verdura, on Pearls

"The pearl — the queen of gems — has a warm and soft, velvety and tactile character. Its natural characteristics exude a sensuous quality that separates the pearl from all other gems.

"While head of the jewelry department at Sotheby's auction house, I had the opportunity to handle a magnificent pearl that, perhaps better than all else, provides a wonderful example of the attraction men feel toward pearls to convey their heartfelt sentiments. It was a famous historical pearl, known as 'La Peregrina' (see Chapter 2). In 1969, Richard Burton acquired it at Sotheby's important jewelry auction as a Valentine's Day present for Elizabeth Taylor (who owns it still); he saw this pearl as the one rare and valuable treasure that could adequately convey his love to Elizabeth.

"The story, however, doesn't end here. The day before the auction there had been some sensational news coverage as the pretender to the Spanish throne claimed ownership of the pearl. I delivered the pearl to the Burtons at Caesar's Palace Hotel in Las Vegas, but only after a bomb scare emptied and delayed my flight. Within minutes of putting the pearl on Elizabeth Taylor's neck, it became lost in the sea of pink shag carpet covering the floor of their vast suite. We were all on our hands and knees crawling around the carpet looking for it when I crawled past a sofa, under which one of Elizabeth's dogs was munching on something. I called Elizabeth, and indeed, the pearl was in the dog's mouth...when recovered, there were only a few small scratches, and who's to say they didn't come from the King of Spain, Mary Tudor, or Napoleon! The pearl was a success with Elizabeth; unfortunately the marriage didn't last, so I suppose it didn't perform the magic Richard was hoping for.

"Throughout history pearls have been the choice of men to bestow upon the ladies of their hearts, and so it remains today. Pearls are a favorite of our clientele, and we love to create pearl jewelry, which as you can see, retains the whimsical character for which Verdura is known.

"At Verdura we use a wide range of colors and shapes, depending upon the look our clients wish to depict — casual and relaxed, understated elegance, or sensual and intimate. Whatever the look, however, we are careful to select only pearls of fine quality, those that will stand the test of time and become treasured heirlooms to be enjoyed, like 'La Peregrina,' for generations to come."

Harry Winston

The firm of Harry Winston is named for its legendary founder, a man who envisioned creating a salon that would become, first and foremost, a showcase for rare gems. The New York salon came to be recognized the world over for incomparable gems set in classic designs amidst a profusion of diamonds. Today, Harry Winston's son continues the quest for rare gems, of rare quality. And pearls are no exception.

Laurence S. Krashes, Vice President of Harry Winston, Inc., on Pearls

"When I think of pearls I think immediately of the first time we ever saw *black* cultured pearls from Tahiti — cultured but naturally colored. They were new, they were unknown, and there were a total of 17 necklaces as assorted pairs in the entire crop. We found them exciting and dramatic, and were so impressed by them that we bought them all! We set them in jewels that legends are made of, and introduced them to the world. The rest is history.

"At Winston we accept only the 'gemmiest' of pearls whose color, luster and lack of blemishes qualify them as unusually rare and valuable, and worthy of inclusion in our inventory. With an international clientele we must also be conscious of the appeal of different colors and lusters in certain parts of the world; our South American clientele, for example, tends to like pearls with shades of gold in them.

"We like to combine pearls with diamonds as they flatter and enhance each other; the luster of the pearls softens the brilliance of the diamonds and yet the brilliance of the diamonds increases and draws one's attention to the luster of the pearl."

Chapter 12

Magnificent Auctions
Highlight Magnificent Pearls

The auction salon has today become a major source of some of the world's finest natural pearls and most important cultured pearls. Major international firms such as Christie's and Sotheby's — both firms dating back to the mid-1700s themselves — and even smaller prestigious firms such as Geneva-based Antiquorum, have brought before the public some of the most magnificent pearls ever known, including some of the "historical" pearls described in Chapter 2. It is worth noting that among rare pearls, the highest price ever paid was in 1988 — $860,000 for a *single, natural* pearl!

Here François Curiel, Head of Christie's Jewelry Division, and John Block, Head of Sotheby's Jewelry Division, share their thoughts on what you should consider when selecting pearls, and describe for us some of the most magnificent pearls handled by their firms in recent years.

Christie's International (founded 1766)

Mr. François Curiel on Pearls

François Curiel is the Head of Christie's International Jewel Sales, Deputy Chairman of Christie's Europe, and Chairman of Christie's Switzerland. As the head of jewelry sales for Christie's offices in New York, Geneva, St. Moritz, London, Amsterdam, and Rome, and having sold the important estate collections of Florence Gould, Marjorie Meriweather Post, Nelson Rockefeller, Joan Crawford, Merle Oberon, Mary Pickford and Caroline Ryan Foulke, he has seen some of the finest pearls in the world.

Advice from François Curiel

"The necessary qualifications affecting the value of a pearl are very similar to those of diamonds. The famous rule of the Four C's, which determines the criteria for valuing diamonds, can therefore be applied in a slightly modified fashion:

"Colour: Whether white, pink, creamy, grey, golden or black, the pearls must have a definite colour or tint. It must be lively and not cloudy or hazy.

"Clarity: A perfectly clear skin, free from scratches, cracks or blemishes of any kind, is highly desirable.

"Cut: Should be fully round, pear or button shaped.

"Carat: Pearls are measured in *millimeters* and *grains*. 1 carat=4 grains; the bigger the better.

"*It is advisable to obtain a certificate of origin (natural or cultured) from any major gemmological laboratory before acquiring pearls.* In the case of cultured pearls the analysis will determine whether the colour is natural or not as this can greatly affect the value."

Magnificent Natural Pearls Sold by Christie's International

La Régente

Sold by Christie's Geneva, May 12, 1988, for $859,100.

Description: Natural egg-shaped pearl of 302.68 grains, suspended from a cushion-shaped diamond acanthus-leaf surmount, in silver and gold (see color section).

History and importance: The Régente pearl, because of its good condition, size, weight and history, holds the world's record price for a *single* natural pearl ever sold at auction.

It was acquired by Napoleon in 1811 for a sum equivalent to $8,000, for his second wife Empress Marie-Louise. It was subsequently given by Napoleon III to his bride-to-be, Eugénie, as a measure of his love! After being kept in hiding for several years during the political unrest in France which began in 1870, "La Régente" — along with most of the French Crown jewels — was sold at auction in 1887, and was acquired by the Russian master jeweler Peter Carl Fabergé (renowned for his gem-studded commemorative eggs), for the equivalent of $35,000. He in turn sold it to the Russian Princess Zenaïde Youssoupov, who often wore it as a pendant to a pearl sautoir or as a hair ornament. Following the Russian Revolution, little is known of La Régente's whereabouts.

The Sara Pearl

Sold by Christie's Geneva, May 21, 1992, for $470,600.

Description: Drop-shaped grey pearl weighing approximately 292 grains, including the pavé-set diamond cap (see color section).

History and importance: The Sara is of high importance because of its size and rare color and because of its mysterious origins. After exhaustive research carried out for Christie's in 1992, we know that this grey pearl is quite likely Jean Baptist Tavernier's "Pearl Number 3" (see Chapter 2). Its home source was the island of Margarita, off the Venezuelan coast. The pearl itself probably weighs about 220 grains (the weight of Tavernier's #3), but over the years the gold cap (weighing 50 to 70 grains) has become part of the pearl and it is impossible to detach it without ruining the pearl.

La Pelegrina

Sold by Christie's Geneva, May 14, 1987, for $463,800.

Description: Pear-shaped pearl of 133.16 grains with rose-cut diamond foliate cap, circular cut diamond surmount.

History and importance: Dating back to the 17th century, La Pelegrina, discussed in greater detail in Chapter 2, was part of the Spanish Crown jewels, and was given by Philip IV to his daughter Maria Teresa on the occasion of her marriage to Louis IV of France. A pearl of this quality, in a size so large, is one of a kind.

La Pelegrina

Princess Tatiana Youssoupoff (1769-1841) wearing La Pelegrina as a single earring.

Natural Pearl Necklace

Sold by Christie's New York, October 26, 1983, for $374,000.

Description: Thirty-two graduated pearls measuring approximately 10.20 to 15.20 mm, the clasp set with an old mine-cut diamond weighing approximately 3.72 carats, and small rose-cut diamonds (see color section).

History and importance: This necklace was originally sold by Bulgari in the 1920s, and over the next fifty years the owner embellished it be replacing individual pearls. In its present composition, the necklace compares in importance with one of the two pearl strands from the Prussian Crown jewels sold in Holland in 1923. Weighing 1765.32 grains, this necklace is the largest to have appeared on the jewelry auction market, and one of exceptional color, brightness, shape and surface perfection.

The Mancini Pearls

Maria Mancini, wearing pearls at her throat, and the Mancini earrings.

Sold by Christie's Geneva, October 2, 1969, for $333,000.

Description: Large drop-shaped pearls with diamond trefoil caps. The drops are detachable, and weigh over 400 grains.

History and importance: The earrings were originally part of the collection of the most powerful Florentine ruling family dei Medici, and were brought to France by Maria dei Medici when she married Henry IV in 1600. Maria passed them to her daughter, Queen Henrietta Maria, as a gift from her family on her wedding to Charles I, King of England. During Charles' troubled reign, most of the Queen's personal jewelry was sold to raise money. She resisted selling her cherished earrings until she became an impoverished, exiled widow, when she finally sold them for enough to keep herself, once again, in style. She sold them to her nephew, King Louis XIV of France, who presented them as a gift to Maria Mancini, niece of Cardinal Mazarin, from which they derived their name. It was rumored in the French court that Louis was passionately in love with Maria and that nothing could more eloquently communicate the depth of his love than these pearls of such rarity and value. Maria ultimately married another, Prince Colonna, in whose family the pearls remained until acquired by an anonymous collector who eventually consigned them to Christie's.

Magnificent Cultured Pearls
Sold by Christie's International

Florence Gould Necklace

Sold by Christie's New York, April 11, 1984, for $990,000.

Description: Designed as a diamond floral vine, suspending pear-shaped graduated South Sea cultured pearls ranging from approximately 12 mm to 16 mm, the floral clasp suspending two diamond and cultured pearl pendants, mounted in platinum *en tremblant*, signed by Alexandre Reza.

History and importance: Pearls so symmetrical and so well matched make this necklace truly spectacular. Florence Gould was born in Los Angeles; her pursuit of the best in pictures, jewelry, furniture, literature, and music is legendary. Gould's collection of jewelry and precious stones stands out as one of the truly great collections of this century, and her pearls were one of the highlights. She is still vividly remembered bedecked in huge pearls as she entertained guests at El Patio, her home at Cannes. Her collection is one of the most outstanding private collections ever sold by Christie's.

Left: The Florence Gould Necklace
Right: Magnificent Triple-Strand Necklace of round, natural black Tahitian cultured pearls, separated by *diamond rondelles* (see Chapter 11, Boucheron)

Three-Strand Black Cultured Pearl Necklace

Sold by Christie's New York, October 24, 1989, for $880,00.

Description: Of 37, 39, and 43 natural black color cultured pearls measuring approximately 12.00 to 15.20 mm, alternating with diamond rondelles, the clasp designed as three oval and circular-cut diamond florets.

History and importance: Natural black pearls are rarer than white pearls and have an unrivaled exotic allure. Limited production, the fact that most of the Tahitian black cultured pearls harvested each season are baroque rather than round, and the increased difficulty in amassing pearls in the same "color" (the shades of black vary dramatically), make complete strands of fine, *matched* round Tahitian black pearls extremely rare.

Sotheby's International (founded 1744)

Mr. John Block on Pearls

Mr. John Block is Executive Vice President and member of the Board of Directors of Sotheby's North and South America. He is in charge of the Jewelry and Precious Objects Division and has supervised every Sotheby's jewelry auction since 1981. He has handled some of the finest pearls in the world from the estates of many prominent people such as Annie-Laurie Aitken, Amelia Peabody, Mrs. Benson Ford, Clare Boothe Luce, Andy Warhol, Ava Gardner, Paulette Goddard, Mrs. Jack Warner and Mrs. Harry Winston.

John Block Comments on Pearls at Auction

"Having set the world record prices for natural pearls, cultured pearls, South Sea cultured pearls and Tahitian black cultured pearls, Sotheby's has discovered that clients mainly look for quality. After the quality factors of color, shape, luster and cleanliness, *size* is the most important factor; size implies importance.

"When buying pearl necklaces, each pearl must be as closely matched as possible, to form a uniform and balanced collection of pearls. The great necklaces which have been sold at auction by Sotheby's all have had a nearly perfect match of pearls.

"The following pearls, all magnificent, illustrate the quality that must be there to command the stellar prices; they also reflect the timelessness and longevity of pearls, and show some of the rare colors that also create attention and excitement."

Magnificent Natural Pearls
Sold by Sotheby's International

Pearl and Diamond Tiara

Sold by Sotheby's Geneva, November 1992, for $645,000.

Description: Designed as a row of pearls alternating with cushion-shaped diamond leaves supporting a row of eight scrolled leaf motifs set with similarly cut diamonds decorated with pearls, surmounted by a large pear-shaped pearl between diamond leafage (see color section).

History and importance: This tiara by Lemonnier was part of the extensive order given to the leading Parisian jewelers by Napoleon III to create jewelry on the occasion of his marriage to Eugénie. In 1887 the French Crown jewels were sold, and in 1890 the tiara was acquired by Prince Albert von Thurn und Taxis as a wedding present for Austrian Archduchess Margarete, whom he married in that year. In recent years the tiara has only been worn on two occasions: by Princess Gloria at her wedding to Prince Johannes von Thurn und Taxis in 1980 and at his sixtieth birthday ball in 1986. Following the Sotheby's sale, this magnificent creation was presented to the Louvre museum in Paris.

La Peregrina

Sold by Sotheby's New York, January 1969, for $37,000.

Description: A pear-shaped drop pearl weighing approximately 203.84 grains suspended from a foliate platinum mount set with numerous old-mine and rose diamonds.

History and importance: This magnificent pearl, discovered in Panama in the mid-16th century, was found in an oyster so small it was nearly thrown away unopened. The pearl was given to Philip II of Spain, and through the centuries it has belonged to royalty throughout Europe (see Chapter 2). It was purchased by Elizabeth Taylor in 1969.

Magnificent Cultured Pearls
Sold by Sotheby's International

Natural Color Black Cultured Pearl
and Diamond Necklace

Sold by Sotheby's New York, April 1990, for $797,500.

Description: A single strand composed of 27 natural color black cultured pearls measuring approximately 17.9 to 13.5 mm, completed by a cluster-form clasp set with round, marquise-shaped, and pear-shaped

Natural Color Black Cultured Pearl
and Diamond Necklace

diamonds weighing approximately 4.75 carats, mounted in platinum, length approximately 17 inches.

History and importance: The natural color black cultured pearl rarely reaches sizes over 14.0 millimeters. Sotheby's has offered several Tahitian pearl necklaces of extremely fine quality and unusual size, but this necklace is, to Sotheby's knowledge, the largest and finest of its kind ever assembled. It brought a record-breaking price of $797,500.

Cultured Pearl and Diamond Necklace

Sold by Sotheby's New York, October 1992, for $2,310,000.

Description: Slightly graduated single strand composed of 23 cultured pearls measuring approximately 20.1 to 16.0 mm, completed by a platinum clasp of spherical form pavé-set with 60 round diamonds weighing approximately 8.25 carats; 17 inches in length (see color section).

History and importance: This necklace is perhaps the ultimate example of pearl "perfection." The first necklace of this quality and size to be offered in a public sale, it broke the world's record price for any cultured pearl necklace ever sold at auction.

Extremely Rare Natural Color Green Cultured Pearl Necklace

Sold by Sotheby's New York, October 1988, for $159,500.

Description: A single strand composed of 31 natural color green cultured pearls graduating from approximately 14.1 to 11.2 mm, completed by a platinum clasp set with 1 marquise-shaped fancy colored "chameleon" diamond weighing 4.54 carats; 17 inches long (see color section).

History and importance: These extraordinary pearls of unusual natural pale silvery-green color are products of Tahitian waters. This is the first strand of round pearls of large size perfectly matched in this highly unusual color, to ever come up for auction. The clasp is composed of a natural color "chameleon" diamond, which changes in color from yellow to green, and complements the rare color of the pearls.

Important Pair of Cultured Pearl and
Diamond Earclips

Important Pair of Cultured Pearl and Diamond Earclips

Sold by Sotheby's New York, April 1989, for $176,000.

Description: Composed of 2 cultured button pearls, each measuring approximately 18.1 by 16.8 mm, simply set in platinum.

History and importance: The spectacular quality of these Australian South Sea cultured pearls, combined with their size, makes these earclips a beautiful treasure.

Part Six
Wearing and Caring for Pearls

Pearls create many moods and reflect the style and individuality of the woman who wears them. Here, contemporary sophistication, and nostalgia and romance.

Chapter 13

Wearing Pearls with Style

Pearls offer more versatility than any other gem — they go well with any style, in any place; they can be worn from morning to evening; they look smart and attractive with sportswear, add an "executive" touch to the business suit, and elegance to even the most glamorous evening gown. Creative stringing, the use of innovative clasps, and wearing pearls in interesting ways with other jewelry can also provide added variety and versatility.

Creative Stringing

Creative stringing can help you create a distinctive look. For the woman who loves color, stringing with other gemstones can create a very personal look. Stringing pearls with gemstone beads such as blue lapis, peach coral, rose quartz, green aventurine, or black onyx, will not only add color but will stretch the budget too. These stones are less expensive than fine pearls, but they complement each other and when strung together create a longer necklace at a lower cost. The beads can be any size — the same size as the pearls, smaller, larger, or assorted sizes — each creating a unique look.

In addition to beads, stringing pearls together with sparkling faceted colored stones or smooth-topped cabochons is a wonderful way to create a look that is distinctly your own. Depending upon the colors used, and the choice of gemstones, the look can be bold and tempestuous, sensual and seductive, or festive and merry, as described in Chapter 11.

Left: Matte white and black sculpted *sterling silver* elements separating Australian South Sea cultured pearls in varying off-round shapes creates a bold look while reducing the overall cost of a "large" necklace.

Right: Australian South Sea keshi pearl necklace with faceted diamonds and rubies randomly interspersed creates dramatic impact (see color section).

Stringing with pearls in *varying sizes* and *shapes* can create a soft, sculptural feeling with gentle movement and harmony. You can even intersperse various colors into the mix. If done in a long necklace, you can also double them, twist them, and create a very important, formal "torsade."

You may need to find your own stringer to put together the right combination to meet your needs; your jeweler should be able to refer you to the right person. Just be sure each bead is separated from each pearl by a knot to avoid their scratching the softer pearl.

Creative Clasps Add Versatility

Innovative pearl clasps that can be inserted or removed when you choose, twisted to create a double strand from one long strand, or add or remove entire sections to create a necklace/bracelet suite, are creating lots of attention today, and presenting interesting new ways to wear pearls.

The *"mystery clasp"* also offers greater versatility. Pearls strung with a "mystery clasp" give the impression of being a continuous pearl necklace with no clasp. It is actually two pearls into which a screw attachment has been inserted; you simply "screw" or "unscrew" the pearls to open or close the strand.

By inserting two mystery clasps into an "opera" length necklace (34-36 inches long), depending upon where the screws are inserted, you can have —

- A continuous, long, opera length necklace

- A princess length necklace, and bracelet (you just unscrew one section to remove it from the necklace and attach it to your wrist)

- A double strand choker necklace (16" and 18")

- A single choker (in either 16" or 18" length)

Depending upon your mood — or the neckline of what you are wearing — you have several options. When you think you would enjoy something more ornate, you can add a brooch, pin, or pearl enhancer to complete the look. Using mystery clasps, one necklace can look like many!

Pearl *shorteners* and *twisters* offer opportunities to wear pearls in a variety of ways, and *pearl enhancers* offer a lovely way to create a different look with pearls, and to use the pearls to highlight another piece of jewelry. Pearl enhancers can be of the pendant type or brooch type.

Innovative interchangeable clasps and pearl enhancers increase versatility.

Be Creative in the Very Way You Wear Your Pearls

Today you can wear your pearls any way you wish. Be bold; be daring. Wear pearl pins on your hats; wear pearls in your hair; wear them draped over the shoulder or down your back with the clasp in front; tie into a gentle knot, or gently twist them! In the historical photos throughout this book, look how women used to wear pearls... we have lots of room to grow! Whatever the event, pearls can create just the right mood.

Today's woman wears pearls in whatever way she chooses.

Cultured Pearls Make Waves with the Well-Dressed Man

Pearls have been used in men's jewelry for centuries, symbolizing power and wealth. From the courts of Europe to the Mogul Empire, no well-dressed man appeared without pearls.

Today men enjoy pearls in a variety of ways — cufflinks, tie tacks, stick pins — and they are especially popular in gentlemen's dress sets.

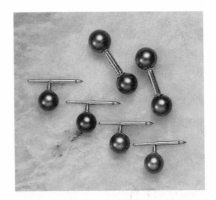

Above: These rare round, natural black color Tahitian cultured pearls make an elegant and distinguished gentleman's dress set. The single black pearl is especially strong and masculine.

Left: Mohammed Ali, Shah of Persia in the early 1900s — wearing the Kajar crown, a pearl masterpiece — knew how to wear pearls!

Few pearls have created as much excitement for men as the natural black pearls from French Polynesia, especially for use in dress sets. The striking, yet simple elegance of the black pearl against the formal white tuxedo shirt or denim jacket makes a statement of strength and confidence.

Designers Move the Pearl into Jewels for Every Occasion

A "string of pearls" has always been the foundation of the classic wardrobe, and no well-dressed woman is ever without them. A magnificent strand of pearls can truly stand on its own, and needs nothing else to draw attention to it; it speaks for itself. But today, a single strand is just the *beginning*!

Pearls are now commanding the attention of the finest designers in the world. They have come to appreciate the subtlety of their shapes and colors, their individuality, and their distinctive character. Most of all, designers recognize the vast possibilities presented by the numerous pearl varieties now available.

Here are a few winning designs from major international design competitions to give you an idea of some of the exciting new looks in pearls, and the new directions in which pearls are moving.

In this wonderful world of pearls there is a pearl waiting for you, for every occasion. And if you're like most, the more you know, the more you see, the more you'll want!

William Richey, USA

Henry Dunay, USA

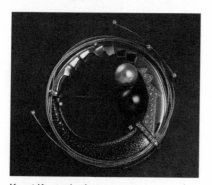

Kaori Kawasake, Japan

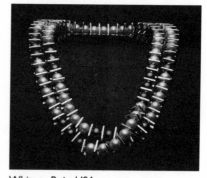

Whitney Boin, USA

Terms Pertaining to Necklaces...

- **Bib** — A necklace of more than three stands of pearls.
- **Collar** (Dog Collar) — Multiple strands of pearls fitting closely around the neck.
- **Graduated** — Necklace containing a large pearl in the center, with pearls becoming progressively smaller toward the ends.
- **Uniform** — Necklace with nearly equal-sized pearls throughout.
- **Rope** (also called "sautoir" or "lariat") — Anything longer than "opera" length, usually over 36 inches.
- **Torsade** — Numerous strands twisted together; usually choker length, but can be longer.

Popular Uniform Necklace Lengths

(All pearls are approximately the same size)

1. **Choker** .... 14-16"
2. **Princess** .... 17-18"
3. **Matinee** .... 20-24"
4. **Opera** .... 30-36"
5. **Rope** .... over 36"

Popular Graduated Necklace Lengths

(Necklaces display larger pearl at center and gradually taper down in size from the front to the back)

Sizes show largest pearl and smallest pearl size.

- **7mm down to 3 1/2 mm** .... 19"
- **8mm down to 4mm** .... 19"
- **9mm down to 6mm** .... 20"

Chapter 14

Caring for Pearls to Keep Them Lustrous

Once you've selected your pearls, proper care is required to protect their beauty. The compact crystalline structure of pearls makes them very durable, but they are soft and this cannot be ignored. Proper care is essential if you want your pearls to keep their lustrous beauty, and pass your treasure on to future generations. Here are some important care tips.

• *Store in a separate pouch* to prevent scratching the pearl's surface on sharp metal edges or prongs, or against harder stones. NEVER TOSS CARELESSLY INTO A PURSE OR TRAVEL CASE. Store or wrap your pearls in a pouch with a soft lining, such as the lovely, inexpensive decorated satin pouches imported today from China. If you don't have anything like this, wrap your pearl jewelry in a linen handkerchief or soft tissue. For temporary storage you can use a plastic bag with a seal to protect them, but do not store pearls in an airtight environment for any extended period of time; pearls need moisture and sealed plastic containers tend to keep out moisture.

• *Avoid contact with these substances* — vinegar, ammonia, and chlorine bleach of any kind, inks, hairspray, perfumes and toilet water, and cosmetics. PUT ON YOUR PEARLS *AFTER* PUTTING ON HAIRSPRAY, PERFUMES AND COSMETICS. These substances will spot or disintegrate the pearl's surface. In strands or necklaces, they can also cause dirt and abrasive substances (found in cosmetics) to cling to the string; if not removed these abrasive particles can cause the pearl to "wear" at the drill hole, not to mention weaken the string and make it more susceptible to breaking.

Be especially careful with vinegar, ammonia, and chlorine. Vinegar is an integral part of salad dressings and a careless drip while eating, onto a pearl ring for example, can have disastrous results. Several years ago a number of pearls in a baroque pearl necklace I was wearing were ruined when a friend unknowingly splattered some salad dressing onto my pearls. Not being aware of it myself — and having done nothing when I removed my pearls except to place them in my jewelry case — I was stunned when several months later I removed them from the jewelry case to find gaping holes in the pearls where the vinegar had *eaten right into them!*

Ammonia can also be deadly to pearls. Keep in mind that many commercial jewelry cleaners contain ammonia, so they should be avoided for pearls. Also, many household cleaners contain ammonia; a friend was wearing a pearl ring at a big jewelry show and didn't think about it as she cleaned the showcase. In addition to "spritzing" the glass, she spritzed her pearl, destroying it.

Finally, remember that chlorine is often used in public swimming pools so never wear your pearl jewelry in a pool.

• *Wipe gently with a **hot damp towel** before putting pearls away* to remove body oils and perspiration — which are particularly harmful to a pearl's color — as well as other damaging substances.

• *Periodic washing is recommended.* Wash gently with a soft cloth in warm, sudsy water using a mild soap (not a detergent). You may also wish to use a soft brush around the knots to be sure they get clean. After washing, rinse them in clear water and then *wrap them in a thin, clean, damp cotton towel to dry* (take a towel like a kitchen towel, wet it and then wring as dry as you can). When the towel is dry, the pearls will be dry, and you will avoid any risk to them. NEVER USE JEWELRY CLEANERS CONTAINING AMMONIA, chemicals containing ammonia or vinegar, or abrasives (cleansers) to clean pearls.

For gummy or caked-on dirt, wipe the pearl, or soak it briefly, in clear fingernail polish remover (the old-fashioned type that is *acetone*). Unlike ammonia and vinegar, acetone will not hurt pearls.

• *Avoid storing pearls in an excessively dry place.* Pearls like moist environments; an excessively dry environment can cause the nacre on your pearls to crack. In Japan, in fact, jewelers place vials of water in their showcases to prevent the hot lamps from creating too dry an environment. *Be especially careful if you store your pearls in a **safety deposit box or vault**.* These areas are very dry. If you use a safety deposit box, place a damp (not wet) cloth in the box with your pearls, and check it periodically and re-dampen it as needed. Don't create an *overly* damp place; too much moisture in a dark environment can cause mildew.

• *Restring pearls periodically.* If they are worn frequently, once a year is recommended. Fine pearls should always be strung with knots tied in the space separating each pearl to prevent them from rubbing against each other (which can damage the nacre), or from scattering and getting lost if the string should accidentally break. One exception is with very small pearls, in which case knotting between each pearl may be aesthetically undesirable. Silk is recommended for stringing.

• *Remove your pearls prior to doing strenuous exercise or work.* Perspiration is detrimental to pearls, but even more important, since the pearl is softer than most other gems, you should be careful to avoid wearing them whenever doing anything that could cause you to scratch or knock them.

• *Avoid ultrasonic cleaners.* These can damage some pearls, especially if the nacre is thin or if there are any surface cracks.

• *Repolishing a damaged pearl may restore its former beauty.* We have had excellent success removing slight pitting, scratches, and some spots from a pearl's surface. They can be easily polished out by using a very *mild* abrasive and a soft chamois cloth — gently rub the pearl with the compound (such as Linde-A polishing compound, available from most lapidary supply houses) and the chamois. You may be pleasantly surprised at how you can restore a slightly damaged pearl to its former beauty. CAUTION: DO NOT DO THIS IF THE PEARL HAS THIN NACRE! THE ABRASIVE WILL REMOVE SOME OF THE NACRE.

Part Seven
Important Advice
Before and After You Buy

Chapter 15

What to Ask When Buying Pearls

The following questions will help you obtain information to help you make better comparisons and choices. Where we have indicated, be sure the information is provided *on the receipt.* Information stated on your receipt provides clear evidence of representations made to you by the seller. In the event of misrepresentation, the written information will enable you to obtain restitution. In the United States, consumer protection laws *require* accurate and complete representation of the facts. If there is misrepresentation, the seller can be held legally liable; in such cases, sellers must refund the purchase price, or deliver a product that meets the written description, REGARDLESS OF THE STORE POLICY (such as "No Return" or "No Credit").

1. **Are these pearls natural, cultured or imitation?** If they are represented to be natural, be sure the words "natural pearls" are stated on your receipt. Also, if natural, pearls should be accompanied by a laboratory report verifying this. If they are not, be sure to get a report (see List of Laboratories in Chapter 17). Note: X-ray examination must be performed to verify that pearls are natural. This must be done by a gem testing laboratory with proper equipment; dental x-rays are unreliable.

2. **What is the shape?** Ask for a statement regarding shape, such as "round," "baroque," "teardrop," and so on. If baroque, note whether symmetrical or asymmetrical. If round, be sure to ask whether the pearl is truly "round" or "three-quarter" round. If round, that should be clearly stated as "round" on the receipt (you may also wish a clarifier, as in "and not three-quarter round").

3. **How would you describe the overall quality of these pearls?** While

there are no universally accepted grading standards, there are general standards that are applied by knowledgeable jewelers; they know whether the pearls they are selling are exceptionally fine, good, average, or poor quality. A statement describing the overall quality should be provided on your receipt. (Where terms such as "AAA" are used, ask for a copy of whatever material the store uses to define their quality distinctions.)

4. **What is the nacre thickness?** Jewelers often don't know the exact thickness, but a knowledgeable jeweler should be able to tell you whether it is thick or thin from the intensity of luster and orient, and be willing to indicate this on your receipt. We recommend knowing what the nacre thickness is; if the jeweler does not know, you can ask that the pearls be submitted to a laboratory to find out prior to purchase. If they do not wish to do so, you may want to make the sale contingent upon the pearls having "thick nacre" and submit them yourself to a laboratory that will grade the nacre thickness (see List of Laboratories in Chapter 17). Note: Black pearls *must* be x-rayed to obtain nacre thickness; even when drilled, nacre thickness cannot be estimated by examination with a loupe or microscope as can be done with "white" or "light" pearls.

5. **Do these pearls have good luster? Do they exhibit "orient"?** Again, find out how the jeweler would grade the luster (exceptionally high or intense, very high, high, medium, fair, poor). Keep in mind that if they exhibit orient, they will probably have very thick nacre.

6. **What color are the pearls?** A knowledgeable jeweler should be able to tell you the *body color* and the *overtone* and provide this information on your receipt; "white-pink," for example, would indicate a white body color with a pink overtone. For fancy-color pearls, the body color, overtone and tone should be given and stated in writing; "dark gold-pink," for example, would describe pearls with a dark-toned golden body color with a pink overtone.

7. **If a fancy-color pearl, is the color natural?** If natural color, this should be stated on the receipt. There should also be a laboratory report accompanying the pearls verifying that the color is natural. Be sure to get the original report, and have the seller write the number and date of the report on your receipt, along with a statement that they are "as described in the accompanying report." If there is no laboratory report, the jeweler can obtain one, or you can ask that the purchase be contingent upon verification of natural color and obtain a laboratory report yourself (see List of Laboratories in Chapter 17). Note: if "natu-

ral color" is written on your receipt, the color *must* be natural; if not, the seller is guilty of misrepresentation.

8. **How does "surface perfection" rank?** Again, there is no universal standard, but a general description such as "exceptional," "very good," "average" and so on, should be indicated on the receipt.

    Sometimes terms such as "flawless," "VVS," "VS," "SI," or "imperfect" are used. VVS indicates "very, very slightly" spotted and corresponds to "very good;" VS indicates "very slightly" spotted and corresponds to "good;" SI indicates "slightly" spotted and corresponds to "good to fair;" and "Imperfect" means heavily spotted and corresponds to "poor."

9. **What size are the pearls? "Is this considered average, large, or small for this type of pearl?"** Remember, price increases as size increases (with each half-millimeter increment). Be sure the exact size is stated on your receipt. When giving the size of pearls in a uniform strand, there is usually a half-millimeter range, that is, "7.0-7.5 mm" or "7.5-8.0" and so on; in a graduated strand, the size of the largest and smallest pearl should be given, as well as an "average" size for the rest.

    Asking how the size compares for the type of pearl you are considering is helpful because it is an indication of rarity—and value—for that type of pearl. A 10 millimeter pearl is not large for a South Sea pearl, for example, but it is extremely large, and very rare, for a Japanese Akoya pearl; a necklace of Akoya pearls in a 10 millimeter size would be *much* more expensive than a comparable necklace of 9 millimeters.

10. **How well matched are the pearls?** This is important to note when buying pearl necklaces, bracelets, or jewelry containing numerous pearls. Poor matching will be noticeable, and such pearls should cost much less than well-matched pearls.

    These questions should enable you to more quickly develop your eye for differences, and decide what is most important to you.

How to Select a Reputable Jeweler

It's very difficult to give advice on selecting a jeweler since there are so many exceptions to any rules we can suggest. Size and years in business are not always indicators of the reliability of a firm. Some one-person jewelry firms are highly respected; others are not. Some well-established firms that have been in business for many years have built their trade on the highest standards of integrity and knowledge; others should have been put out of business years ago.

One point worth stressing is that for the average consumer, price alone is not a reliable indicator of the integrity or knowledge of the seller. Aside from variations in quality, which often are not readily discernible to the consumer, significant price differences can also result from differences in jewelry manufacturing processes. Many jewelry manufacturers sell mass-produced lines of good quality jewelry to jewelers all over the country. Mass-produced items, many of which reflect beautiful, classic designs, are usually much less expensive than hand-made, one-of-a-kind pieces, or those on which there is a limited production. The work of some designers may be available in only a few select establishments, and may carry a premium because of skill, labor, reputation, and limited distribution. Handmade or one-of-a-kind pieces are always more expensive since the initial cost of production is paid by one individual rather than shared by many, as in mass-produced pieces.

Furthermore, depending upon the store, retail markups also vary, based on numerous factors unique to each retailer, including differences in insurance coverage, security costs, credit risks, education and training costs, special services such as in-house design and custom jewelry production and repair, customer service policies, and more.

The best way to select wisely is by shopping around. Go to several fine jewelry firms in your area and compare the services they offer, how knowledgeable the salespeople seem, the quality of their products, and pricing for specific items. This will give you a sense of what is fair in your market area. As you do so, however, remember to ask the right questions to be sure the items are truly comparable, and pay attention to design and manufacturing differences as well. As part of this process, it may be helpful to consider these questions:

- **How long has the firm been in business?** A quick check with the Better Business Bureau may reveal whether or not there are significant consumer complaints.

- **What are the gemological credentials of the jeweler, manager, or owner?** Do they have any special expertise where pearls are concerned?

- **What special services are provided?** Are custom design services, rare or unusual pearls, or educational programs available?

- **How would you describe the overall appearance and atmosphere?** Is the jewelry nicely displayed and the manner of the staff professional and helpful? Or hustling, pushy or intimidating?

- **What is the store's policy regarding returns?** Full refund or only store credit? How many days? On what basis can jewelry be returned?

- **What is the repair or replacement policy?**
- **Will the firm allow a piece to be taken "on memo"?** It won't hurt to ask. Some jewelers will. However, unless you know the jeweler personally this is not often permitted today because of increased security risk and insurance company requirements.
- **To what extent will the firm guarantee its merchandise to be as represented?** Be careful here. Make sure you've asked the right questions and get complete and accurate information on the bill of sale, or you may find yourself stuck because of a technicality.

If the jeweler can't or won't provide the necessary information, we recommend you go to another store, no matter how much you've fallen in love with the piece. And, if you're making the purchase on a contingency basis, put the terms of the contingency on the bill of sale.

Never allow yourself to be intimidated into accepting anyone's claims. Beware of the person who says "Just trust me" or who tries to intimidate you with statements such as "Don't you trust me?" A trustworthy jeweler will not have to ask for your trust; he or she will earn it through knowledge, reliability, and a willingness to give you information you request — in writing.

Again, in general, you will be in a stronger position to differentiate between a knowledgeable, reputable jeweler and one who isn't if you've taken time to learn as much as possible about pearls and taken time to visit several jewelers to compare. Unless you are an expert, visit several fine jewelry firms, ask questions, examine merchandise carefully, and *then* be the judge.

Chapter 16

Good Insurance Requires
a Good Appraisal

Fine pearls are very expensive. It's important to get a thorough appraisal on them to ensure that you have adequate coverage in the event of loss, damage, or theft. This is especially important in cases when the insurance company can exercise a *replacement* option rather than reimburse the full value of your policy; a thorough appraisal will provide the insurer with adequate information to replace lost or damaged pearls with pearls which really are of "comparable quality."

A pearl appraisal should be more than an estimate of current retail value. In addition to value it should include verification that the pearls are genuine and not imitation, and provide a complete description of quality. A thorough appraisal will help you get appropriate insurance, ensure replacement with "like kind," and serve as positive identification if lost or stolen pieces are recovered. When appropriate, the appraiser can also submit your pearls to a gem testing laboratory to confirm essential information and obtain necessary documentation regarding whether pearls are natural or cultured, the origin of color, and nacre thickness, for example.

A pearl appraisal should include a description of what type of jewelry it is (necklace, ring, etc.), and fully describe the setting, type of clasp, and quality of pearls and other stones in the piece. In describing the pearls themselves, the appraisal must state whether or not the pearls are cultured or natural, and describe the type of pearl (round, freshwater, South Sea, etc.), its color, intensity of luster and orient, skin texture, shape, degree of roundness, and size of pearls. For necklaces, it should also provide the number of strands, length of each strand, number of pearls in each strand, whether or not knotted, and describe the matching of the pearls in each strand. In graduated strands, it should also provide the measurement of the largest (center) pearl, and each small pearl at the ends of the strand, and indicate how evenly graduated they are.

Look for a qualified, independent gemologist-appraiser to do the appraisal.

Selecting an Independent Laboratory or Gemologist-Appraiser

There are essentially no officially established guidelines for going into the gem appraising business or opening a laboratory. Anyone can represent himself as an "appraiser." While many highly qualified professionals are in the business, some others lack the expertise to offer these services. So it is essential to select an appraiser or laboratory with care and diligence. Further, if the purpose of the appraisal or report is to verify genuineness and quality, we recommend that you deal with someone who is in the business of gem identification and appraising, and not primarily in the business of selling gems.

To be a qualified gemologist or gemologist-appraiser requires extensive formal training and experience. You must look for specific credentials to be sure the person you select has the proper training. Pearls may require special expertise to properly value, so you should also inquire about the appraiser's experience in evaluating your particular type of pearls.

Look for specific credentials. The Gemological Institute of America and gemological associations around the world such as the Gemmological Association of Great Britain award internationally recognized diplomas. G.I.A.'s highest award is GG (Graduate Gemologist) and the Gemmological Association of Great Britain awards the FGA—Fellow of the Gemmological Association (FGAA in Australia; FCGA in Canada). Some hold this honor "With Distinction." In Germany, the DGG is awarded; in Asia, the AG. Make sure the gemologist you select has one of these diplomas.

Check the gemologist's length of experience. In addition to formal training, to be reliable a gemologist needs extensive experience in the handling of gems, use of the equipment necessary for accurate identification and evaluation, and activity in the marketplace. For pearls, a gemologist should have at least several years' experience in a well-equipped laboratory, and regular exposure to a wide range of cultured and natural pearls.

The following organizations are well respected in the United States, and can assist you in finding a reliable independent laboratory or gemologist-appraiser in your community.

The American Society of Appraisers
P.O. Box 17265
Washington, DC 20041
(703) 478-2228
Ask for a current listing of *Master Gemologist Appraisers*

The American Gem Society
8881 West Sahara
Las Vegas, NV 89117
(702) 255-6500
Ask for a list of *Independent Certified Gemologists or Certified Gemologist Appraisers*

The Accredited Gemologists Association
3309 Juanita Street
San Diego, CA 92105
(619) 286-6614
Ask for a list of *Certified Gem Laboratories* or *Certified Master Gemologists*

Chapter 17

Getting a Laboratory Report

In addition to an appraisal from a good gemologist-appraiser, we recommend that anyone buying fine pearls—cultured or natural—obtain a report from a respected laboratory, even though pearl reports are not routinely issued at this time. A good gemologist can confirm quality and value, but most lack the equipment necessary to confirm whether or not pearls are natural, and to detect sophisticated treatments.

When selecting a laboratory, it is important to find out what information is provided on the report. As you can see from the sample reports shown here, the type of information provided varies from one laboratory to another, as do charges for services depending upon what the report covers. Normally the fee is modest; any respected lab will be happy to provide you with a list of the pearl services they provide and the charges for each.

Most major laboratories will perform a variety of sophisticated tests for pearl *identification*, including x-radiography, to determine the type of pearl (natural, cultured, imitation, conch, abalone, and so on). In addition, the report normally provides information regarding *size/ weight, shape, color,* and *number of pearls* (in strands or pieces with more than one). In the case of fancy-color cultured or natural pearls—black, golden, green, and so on—the report should indicate *whether or not the color is natural or treated;* if treated, some laboratories will indicate by what means (the manner by which a pearl is color enhanced is usually not something that consumers need to know; it is enough to know the color is not natural).

We highly recommend obtaining a report, if possible, from a laboratory that will provide information regarding ***nacre thickness*** although this is not yet provided by most laboratories (see list below). Given the relationship between nacre thickness and the pearl's longevity, this is essential information for any important piece of cultured pearl jewelry.

An independent lab or experienced gemologist-appraiser can provide a reliable assessment of nacre thickness for drilled pearls when the drill hole is visible; if undrilled, most can provide a general indication of thickness based on visual appearance, and point out dangerously thin nacre. Sophisticated laboratory testing is necessary, however, when it is difficult to examine the drill hole or if the pearl is undrilled.

A laboratory report is essential to determine exact nacre thickness, whether pearls are natural, and whether or not color is natural. The gemologist appraiser can add to this information a full quality assessment, including luster, surface perfection, shape, and color, and estimate the value of the pearls (major labs don't provide information pertaining to value). In the case of white Akoya cultured pearls, an increasing number of independent appraising laboratories and gemologist-appraisers are using a "master" grading set of pearls such as the "G.I.A. Gem Pearl Master Comparison Set" and the "I.G.I. Cultured Pearl Grading Master Comparison Set."

A laboratory report on your pearls combined with a quality evaluation by an independent gemologist-appraiser can be invaluable in confirming representations that may have been made by the seller, or equally important, in the absence of any quality representation. Remember: Retailers use their own systems, based on the quality they sell; "AAA" quality refers to the best that particular retailer has; it may be the equivalent of a "B" quality from another retailer. An independent gemologist-appraiser can help you understand how the quality of your pearls would be graded in general—exceptionally rare, excellent, very good, good, fair, poor, very poor.

If there is no convenient laboratory or gemologist-appraiser, you can request that the jeweler submit them to the laboratory of your choice, on your behalf. Or, if you are not uncomfortable entrusting the pearls to an unknown party, valuable items can be sent everywhere in the United States by *registered, insured U.S. mail.* This is how most gems and jewelry are sent from one location to another.

International Laboratories Issuing Pearl Reports

The laboratories on the following selected list issue reports that provide information on pearl identity (natural, cultured, imitation) and origin of color (natural, treated) as well as size, weight, color and shape.

Several of these laboratories also describe nacre thickness; where this is the case, it is so indicated. Some provide nacre thickness only if requested, and this is also indicated. One of the following also provides, in addition to nacre thickness, grades for other important quality factors.

Since nacre thickness and quality issues are becoming such important concerns, an increasing number of laboratories are adding these services, and they may become available from laboratories listed below that are not offering the service at this time. When seeking laboratory services for pearls, please check directly with the laboratory in question to learn what services are available.

Key to Services Offered by Laboratories Listed

- A = Basic report indicating identity (natural, cultured, imitation), size/weight, color, shape.

- B = Basic report, *plus description of nacre thickness* (i.e. "Thick," "Medium," "Very Thin" and so on); some laboratories provide actual nacre thickness, in millimeters (if so, this is indicated).

- C = Quality report, including basics, plus nacre thickness, and *grading of luster, surface perfection, shape, and matching* (in strands).

- T = Provide reports to "*the trade*" only (in such cases, you can request that the jeweler obtain a report for you).

Selected List of International Laboratories Issuing Pearl Reports

United States

Gemological Institute of America
G.I.A. Gem Trade Laboratory
580 Fifth Avenue
New York, NY 10036
(212) 221-5858

1630 Stewart Street
Santa Monica, CA 90404
(310) 828-3148
Pearl reports: A

International Gemmological Institute
579 Fifth Avenue
New York, NY 10036
(212) 753-7100
Pearl reports: A, B (if drilled), C

Great Britain

Gem Testing Laboratory of Great Britain
27 Greville Street
(Saffron Hill Entrance)
London EC1N 8SU
England
(44) (171) 405-3351
Pearl reports: A, B (upon request), T

Japan

Central Gem Laboratory
15-14 Ueno 5-Chome
Taito-ku, Tokyo 110
Japan
(81) (3) (3836) 3219
Pearl reports: A, T

Switzerland

Gubelin Gemological Laboratory
Maihofstrasse 102
CH-6000 Lucerne 9
Switzerland
(41) (41) 261717
Pearl reports: A, B (verbally, on request)

SSEF Swiss Gemological Institute
Falknerstrasse 9
CH-4001 Basel
Switzerland
(41) (61) 262-0640
Pearl reports: A, B (upon request)

Thailand

Asian Institute of Gemological Sciences
919/1 Silom Road, Jewelry Trade Center
South Tower, 11th Floor
Bangkok 10500
Thailand
(66) (2) 267-4315-9
Pearl reports: A, B — provides nacre thickness, in mm.

ASIAN INSTITUTE OF GEMOLOGICAL SCIENCES

Gemstone Identification, Grading, and Research Laboratory
12/1 Surasak Road, Suagrak, Bangkok 10500, Thailand
Tel:(662)237 3600-5   Fax:(662)238 3905

PEARL IDENTIFICATION REPORT

Report number: P-9506025   Date: June 19, 1994

Client number: SAMPLE

Unless otherwise indicated, the item(s) described below has/have been examined by at least two
qualified AIGS staff gemologists and the stated result obtained. This report is limited in accordance
with the agreement printed on its inside front cover, the cover being an integral part of this report:

Item(s)

> One undrilled near round silver white "pearl" weighing 4.72cts and measuring approximately
> 8.85 - 8.80 x 8.16mm.

Result(s):

> Found to be a CULTURED PEARL.

Comment(s):

> Approximate nacre thickness 0.92mm.

Photograph of item(s) examined - not actual size

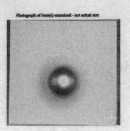

For and on behalf of

The Asian Institute of Gemological Sciences

Sample Asian Institute of Gemological Sciences Pearl Identification Report

SCHWEIZERISCHES GEMMOLOGISCHES INSTITUT

INSTITUT SUISSE DE GEMMOLOGIE

SWISS GEMMOLOGICAL INSTITUTE

SSEF

Falknerstrasse 9
CH-4001 **Basel** / Switzerland

Telephone 061 / 262 0640
Telefax   061 / 262 0641
Postcheck 80-15013-2

TEST REPORT No. Sample

on the authenticity of the following pearls

Shape:	one strand of 120 round to roundish, drilled pearls
Total weight :	approximately 32.23 grams (including thread and clasp with diamonds)
Measurements:	approximately 3.90 - 5.40 - 8.05 - 5.45 - 4.00 mm
Total length:	approximately 73 cm
Colour:	slightly cream to slightly rosé
Identification:	regularly graduated necklace of 119 N A T U R A L P E A R L S and 1 C U L T U R E D P E A R L (Nr 57 from the clasp)

SSEF - SWISS GEMMOLOGICAL INSTITUTE
Gemstone Testing Division

Basel, 16 March 1995 ls

L. Kiefert, Dipl.-Min.

Dr. H.A. Hänni, FGA

Only the original report with the official embossed stamp is a valid identification document for the described pearls.

Sample SSEF Laboratory Report

INTERNATIONAL GEMMOLOGICAL INFORMATION

A Division of International Gemmological Institute, Inc.

579 Fifth Avenue
New York, New York 10017
(212) 753-7100
Telefax (212) 753-7759

1/7 Schupstraat
B-2000 Antwerp, Belgium
03-2316845
Telex 35226 IGI B

CULTURED PEARL GRADING REPORT   June 1, 1994

THE FOLLOWING WERE, AT THE TIME OF THE EXAMINATION, THE CHARACTERISTICS
OF THE ARTICLE(S), BASED UPON GENERALLY ACCEPTED GRADING TECHNIQUES.

DESCRIPTION OF ARTICLE(S): ONE NECKLACE WITH ONE 14 KARAT YELLOW GOLD CLASP, STAMPED
"14 K", MEASURING IN OVERALL LENGTH 18", CONTAINING 102 CULTURED PEARLS, DETAILED
DESCRIPTION BELOW:

COLOR DESCRIPTION
Body Color .... WHITE
Overtone............ ROSE'
Orient .... NONE

LUSTER .... HIGH

NACRE THICKNESS .... VERY THICK

BLEMISHES/SPOTTING .... LIGHTLY SPOTTED

SHAPE .... ROUND IN ALL

MAKE/MATCHING .... GOOD

COMMENTS:

ENLARGED TO SHOW DETAIL

INTERNATIONAL GEMMOLOGICAL INFORMATION

By

NOTICE: SEE TERMS AND CONDITIONS ON REVERSE
SEE APPENDIX A

NY SPECIMEN

Sample International Gemmological Information Cultured Pearl Grading Report

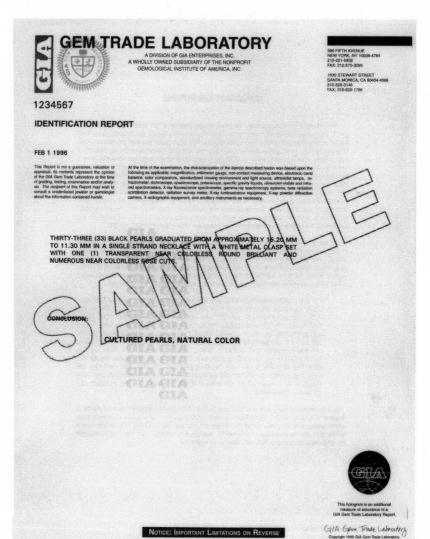

GEM TRADE LABORATORY

A DIVISION OF GIA ENTERPRISES, INC.
A WHOLLY OWNED SUBSIDIARY OF THE NONPROFIT
GEMOLOGICAL INSTITUTE OF AMERICA, INC.

580 FIFTH AVENUE
NEW YORK, NY 10036-4794
212-221-5858
FAX: 212-575-3095

1630 STEWART STREET
SANTA MONICA, CA 90404-4088
310-829-3148
FAX: 310-829-1790

1234567

IDENTIFICATION REPORT

FEB 1 1996

This Report is not a guarantee, valuation or appraisal. Its contents represent the opinion of the GIA Gem Trade Laboratory at the time of grading, testing, examination and/or analysis. The recipient of this Report may wish to consult a credentialed jeweler or gemologist about the information contained herein.

At the time of the examination, the characterization of the item(s) described herein was based upon the following as applicable: magnification, millimeter gauge, non-contact measuring device, electronic carat balance, color comparators, standardized viewing environment and light source, ultraviolet lamps, refractometer, dichroscope, spectroscope, polariscope, specific gravity liquids, ultraviolet-visible and infrared spectrometers, X-ray fluorescence spectrometer, gamma-ray spectroscopy systems, beta radiation scintillation detector, radiation survey meter, X-ray luminescence equipment, X-ray powder diffraction camera, X-radiographic equipment, and ancillary instruments as necessary.

THIRTY-THREE (33) BLACK PEARLS GRADUATED FROM APPROXIMATELY 15.20 MM TO 11.30 MM IN A SINGLE STRAND NECKLACE WITH A WHITE METAL CLASP SET WITH ONE (1) TRANSPARENT NEAR COLORLESS ROUND BRILLIANT AND NUMEROUS NEAR COLORLESS ROSE CUTS.

CONCLUSION:

CULTURED PEARLS, NATURAL COLOR

This hologram is an additional measure of assurance of a GIA Gem Trade Laboratory Report.

GIA Gem Trade Laboratory

Copyright 1995 GIA Gem Trade Laboratory

NOTICE: IMPORTANT LIMITATIONS ON REVERSE

Sample GIA Gem Trade Laboratory Report

Where to Go for Additional Information

Cultured Pearl Information Center
321 East 53rd St.
New York, NY 10022

Jewelry Information Center
19 W. 44th St.
New York, NY 10036

The Pearl Society
623 Grove St.
Evanston, IL 60201

South Sea Pearl Consortium Ltd.
c/o Evins Communications Ltd.
635 Madison Ave.
New York, NY 10022

Tahitian Pearl Association
580 Fifth Ave., 21st Fl.
New York, NY 10036

World Pearl Organization
Japan Pearl Promotion Society
Shinju-kaikan, 3-6-15
Kyobashi, Chuo-ku
Tokyo, Japan 104

  In addition to the associations above, the following is an excellent international pearl journal —

"Pearl World"
1822 West Glendale Avenue, Suite 401
Phoenix, Arizona 85021-8543

Selected Readings

Ball, S.H. *The Mining of Gems and Ornamental Stones by American Indians.* Washington, D.C.: Smithsonian Institution, Anthropological Papers No. 13, 1941. Information here shows that pearls were highly valued by native Americans.

Ball, S.H. *A Roman Book on Precious Stones.* Los Angeles: Gemological Institute of America, 1950. Fascinating insights into the high value—monetary and otherwise—of pearls during the Roman period.

Bradford, E. *Four Centuries of European Jewelry.* London: Country Life, Ltd., 1967. Interesting historical insights.

Budge, Sir E. A. Wallis. *Amulets & Talismans.* New Hyde Park, N.Y.: University Books, 1961. Interesting lore and mythology.

Cavenago-Bignami Moneta, S. *Gemmologia.* Milan: Heopli, 1965. One of the most extensive works on gems available, with outstanding section on pearls. Excellent photography. Available in the Italian language only.

Evans, Joan. *A History of Jewelry 1700-1870.* London: Faber and Faber, 1953. Especially interesting for the antique jewelry collector.

Farn, Alexander E. *Pearls: Natural, Cultured and Imitation.* Oxford: Butterworth-Heinemann Ltd., 1991. A complete and thorough work, for amateur and professional alike.

Kunz, G. F. *The Curious Lore of Precious Stones.* Reprint, with *The Magic of Jewels and Charms,* New York: Dover Publications, 1972. Excellent source of information on the lore and mythology that surround pearls.

———— and Stevenson. *The Book of the Pearl.* 1908. Reprint, New York: Dover Publications, 1993. The most lavish and comprehensive book on pearls ever written and filled with amazing information, especially on natural pearls (although some of the information has been disproved in modern times).

Lintilhac, Jean-Paul. *Black Pearls of Tahiti.* English trans. J.L. Sherman. Tahiti: Royal Tahitian, 1985. Exceptional photography and fascinating look into the black pearl, and the island paradise from which it comes.

Matlins, Antoinette L. & Bonanno, A.C. *Jewelry & Gems: The Buying Guide.* Woodstock, Vt.: GemStone Press, 1993. A non-technical book that has an excellent section on pearls.

———. *Engagement & Wedding Rings: The Definitive Buying Guide for People in Love.* Woodstock, Vt.: GemStone Press, 1990. Excellent section on pearls, especially as adornment of the bride.

Salomon, Paule & Roudnitska, Michel. *Tahiti: The Magic of the Black Pearl.* Papeete: Tahiti Perles (Papeete) & Times Editions, Singapore, 1987. A magical journey into the land and the very heart of the black pearl. Many of the photographs are truly art.

Shirai, Shohei. *Pearls and Pearl Oysters of the World.* Okinawa: Marine Planning Company, 1994. In English and Japanese, a superb presentation of photographs of different oysters and the pearls they produce. Excellent resource, especially for the professional.

Twining, Lord. *A History of the Crown Jewels of Europe.* London: Batsford, 1962. Excellent resource that highlights some of the fine natural pearls among the Crown jewels.

Zucker, Benjamin. *Gems and Jewels — A Connoisseur's Guide.* New York: Thames and Hudson, Inc., 1984. Excellent section on pearls in this lavishly illustrated book on the history and use of "great" gemstones of the world, giving fascinating historical facts and mythological tidbits as well as many examples of the jeweler's art from widely differing cultures.

A Practical Pearl Glossary

As you shop, here is a working vocabulary to help you better understand what you are seeing, and describe what you want.

Abalone — A univalve mollusc known for its iridescent natural pearls, for its shell (which is widely used for ornamentation), and for its meat (increased fishing for the latter has seriously depleted the number of abalone).

Akoya — A pearl produced by the Japanese "Akoya" oyster; this oyster is also called "*Pinctada martensii*" or "*Pinctada fucata.*"

Ama — The diving girls in Japan who originally dove for the oysters; now a tourist attraction.

Aragonite — A form of calcium carbonate, which constitutes a large portion of the pearl.

Baroque — A pearl with an irregular shape.

Bivalve mollusc — A mollusc with a pair of shells (valves) which open by means of a hinge.

Biwa pearl — A non-nucleated cultured pearl from Japan's largest lake, Lake Biwa.

Cleanliness — Absence of blemishes (spots, pimples, cracks) or discoloration on the pearl's surface. Also referred to as the pearl's "surface perfection" or simply "perfection."

Conchiolin — The first layer secreted by a mollusc to ease the discomfort caused when a foreign substance gets lodged in the mantle tissue. Usually light brownish, but can be almost black. It is a highly porous material, similar to our fingernails, and is especially important because it binds the nacre together to form the pearl.

Conch pearls — Not truly a "pearl" but a lovely, rare and valuable product of the giant conch, a univalve mollusc. Pink is the most desired color. They often exhibit a "flame" pattern on their surface.

Cultivated pearl — Another term used to indicate "*cultured* pearl."

Domé® pearl — A solid blister pearl grown around a mother-of-pearl nucleus on the inside of the mollusc shell; when removed, part of the surrounding shell remains. It is a very distinctive looking pearl, resembling a mabé with its domed shape, but much more interesting in appearance, and much more durable.

Fluorescence — Normally invisible wavelengths of light that become "visible" when exposed to ultraviolet radiation. When placed under a lamp which provides ultraviolet light (these lamps provide both "long-wave" and "short-wave" radiation) you will be able to see in pearls a color or colors not seen (invisible) otherwise. Gems or pearls that exhibit color under ultraviolet light — color not seen in normal light — are exhibiting "fluorescence." The color(s) of the fluorescence, and whether or not it is the same under both long- and short-wave radiation, can be helpful in identifying natural and cultured pearls.

Freshwater pearl — Pearls produced by *margaritifera* freshwater molluscs.

Grain — The standard unit of weight once used for natural pearls. Four grains are equal to one carat. Carat weight is now generally used.

Gold-lip oyster — A large oyster (var. of *Pinctada maxima*) used in some countries to produce South Sea cultured pearls; it is called a "yellow lip" because it produces a yellowish nacre, and pearls that typically range from off-white to rich, deep gold in color.

Half-drilled — Pearls which have only been partly drilled, as for rings or earrings. These pearls sell for more (per pearl) than pearls which are fully drilled, as those used in necklaces.

Harlequin pearls — *Untreated* round Chinese freshwater cultured pearls in a variety of natural colors strung together.

Kan — A Japanese commercial unit of weight; equals 1000 momme.

Keshi — Japanese word meaning something as tiny as you can imagine, such as a grain of sand; used originally for very tiny pearls that resulted by accident as part of the culturing process; now used to refer to all-nacre baroque pearls produced when something goes wrong in the process of culturing a pearl; technically not a "natural" pearl, but virtually identical to natural baroques. South Sea keshi can be very large; Japanese keshi can be miniscule. Both types are becoming rare.

Luster — The unique, internally emanating "glow" that distinguishes the pearl from all other gems. It is created by the refraction and reflection of light through microscopic crystals which form in the pearl nacre. Thin coated or imitation pearls may possess a surface shine, but they do not absorb and refract rays of light, so they lack the depth and reflective character of good luster.

Mabé pearl — Produced by the oyster *Pteria penguin*; an "assembled" pearl created by *filling* a hollow blister and then applying a mother-of-pearl back to complete the "pearl." Usually hemispherical. Fragile.

Margaritifera — The freshwater *margaritifera* mussel is used to culture freshwater pearls; the *Pinctada margaritifera* is a saltwater pearl-producing oyster, and the black-lip variety is used to produce naturally black color South Sea cultured pearls. There is also a white-lip and a yellow-lip variety being used in cultured pearl production.

Millimeter — A unit of measure, used to determine the diameter and overall measurements of a pearl. Approximately $\frac{1}{25}$th of an inch.

Momme — Japanese weight measurement used for pearls. One momme equals 3.75 grams, or 18.75 carats.

Nacre — The usually whitish crystalline substance which the mollusc secretes around a foreign "intruder" and which forms what we know as the pearl (as concentric layers of this substance build up over time).

Nucleus — The "irritant" embedded by man into a pearl mollusc, around which the oyster secretes nacre, which builds up to form the pearl.

Orient — The shimmering, irridescent play-of-color seen on or just below the surface of the pearl, resulting from the interplay of light within the microscopic crystals produced in the nacre.

Oriental pearl — A *natural* pearl; this term is reserved for use *only* when referring to natural pearls.

Pinctada — Refers to a pearl-producing oyster genus. Usually abbreviated to "*P.*"; for example, *P. fucata* would indicate the *Pinctada* genus and the *fucata* species.

P. fucata — Also known as *P. martensii*, the oyster used to produce cultured Japanese and Chinese pearls (see below).

P. maxima — A large oyster used to produce South Sea cultured pearls; includes the "silver lip" which produces the silvery white varieties typical of Australia, and the "yellow lip" which can produce yellow and golden pearls.

P. martensii — A pearl-producing oyster used in Japan and China; smaller than *P. maxima*, capable of producing pearls up to a maximum size of about 10+ millimeters.

P. margaritifera — Pearl-producing oyster with black, white, or golden colored "lips," producing nacre similar in color to its "lips." The black-lip variety is used in Tahiti and other parts of French Polynesia to produce natural color black cultured pearls.

Pteria penguin — Mollusc used to produce mabé pearls.

Seed pearls — Tiny natural pearls weighing under $\frac{1}{4}$ grain, usually less than 2 millimeters in diameter.

Credits

Grateful acknowledgment is made to the many individuals and organizations who contributed photographs for use in this book.

2, t.l. & t.r.: The Royal Collection © Her Majesty Queen Elizabeth II. b.: Kunz and Stevenson, *The Book of the Pearl*, 1908.
7, l.: Kunz. r: Cultured Pearl Information Center.
9: Kunz.
13: Mikimoto U.S.A.
15: Sotheby's International.
17: Kunz.
20: Kunz.
22: Broome Pearls Pty., Ltd., Australia.
23: K. Scarratt, AIGS.
28, l.: Andy Muller, Golay Buchel. r.: Yamakatsu Pearl Co., Ltd.
31: K. Scarratt, AIGS.
34: Antoinette Matlins.
36: K. Scarratt, AIGS.
39: Yamakatsu Pearl Co., Ltd.
40: Cultured Pearl Information Center.
41, l.: Andy Muller, Golay Buchel. r: ©Eve J. Alfillé, Ltd. (Photo: Russ & Mary Olsson.)
43: American Pearl Co.
44: American Pearl Co.
45, t.l.: Henry Dunay. t.r.: Mikimoto U.S.A. b.l.: K. Scarratt, AIGS. b.r.: Yamakatsu Pearl Co., Ltd.
46: Andy Muller, Golay Buchel.
47: American Pearl Co.
48: Kunz.
49: ©T. Ardai.
50: Yamakatsu Pearl Co., Ltd.
55: Kunz.
68: K. Scarratt, AIGS.
69: Yamakatsu Pearl Co., Ltd.
71: Yamakatsu Pearl Co., Ltd.
73, t.l. & t.r.: Yamakatsu Pearl Co., Ltd. b.l.: ©Patti J. Geolat. b.r.: ©T. Ardai.
74: Yamakatsu Pearl Co., Ltd.
Part 5: Photos courtesy of the contributors.
158: Cultured Pearl Information Center.
160, l.: Paspaley Pearling. r.: Asprey.

161: Eberle.
162: Cultured Pearl Information Center.
163, l.: Kunz. r.: Antoinette Matlins.
164, t.l.: William Richey. t.r.: Henry Dunay. b.l.: Kaori Kawasake. b.r.: Whitney Boin.

Color Section
Page 1, clockwise from top left: K. Scarratt, AIGS. Henry Dunay. Andy Muller, Golay Buchel. ©Bill Kalina. Pacific Coast Pearls. Yamakatsu Pearl Co., Ltd. ©Patti J. Geolat.
Page 2: Asprey. Inset: Antiquorum Fine Auctioneers, Geneva.
Page 3, clockwise from top: Yamakatsu Pearl Co., Ltd. Broome Pearls. ©Patti J. Geolat.
Page 4, "Freshwater Cultured Pearls from America": American Pearl Co. "Pearls from China," clockwise from top right: K. Scarratt, AIGS. ©Trio. ©P. Crevoshay.
Page 5, "Pearls from Japan," clockwise from top: ©T. Ardai. ©Eve J. Alfillé, Ltd. Mikimoto U.S.A.
Page 6, "Pearls from Australia," clockwise from top: Albert Asher Co. Yamakatsu Pearl Co., Ltd. Andy Muller, Golay Buchel.
Page 7, "Pearls from Tahiti," clockwise from top: Andy Muller, Golay Buchel. Tahiti Perles. Antoinette Matlins.
Page 8, "Pearls from Indonesia & the Phillippines," clockwise from top left: ©T. Ardai. Jewelmer International Corp. Mikimoto U.S.A. "Pearls from the Cook Islands," clockwise from top right: Island Images, The Cook Islands. Island Images, The Cook Islands. © Lucius Hastings. © Lucius Hastings.
Pages 9-16: Photos courtesy of the jewelers and auction houses cited.

Front Cover
Second Row l.: Courtesy Benjamin Zucker. r.: Broome Pearls.
Third Row center: ©T. Ardai. r.: Pacific Coast Pearls.
Bottom: Asprey.

Christie's research information compiled by Esmeralda Spinola, intern in Christie's Geneva Jewellery Department, 1994, was used as a resource for Chapter 12.

Thanks to Joan Rolls and Island Images for their assistance in providing information on and photos of Cook Island pearls.

A
abalone pearls, 52–53
Accredited Gemologists
    Association, The, 178
Akhito, Emperor of Japan,
    141
Akoya pearls
    about, 39, 50
    artificial enhancements, 79
    experts' advice, 123
    quality, value and, 65, 74,
    92, 95–96
Alfillé, Eve J., 113–114
American freshwater pearls
    about, 43–44
    artificial enhancements, 78
    price charts, 101
    quality, value and, 65,
    98–99
American Gem Society, The,
    178
American Society of
    Appraisers, The, 178
ammonia, pearls and, 166,
    167
Anthony and Cleopatra,
    14–15
appraisals, insurance,
    176–178
aragonite, 24
Asia, pearls and, 5–6, 7
Asian Institute of Gemological
    Sciences, 182, 183
Assael, Salvador, 114
asymmetrical pearls, 39
aubergine pearls, 93
auctions, pearl, 148–156
Australia, pearls and, 90–91,
    124–127
authenticity, certificate of,
    116

B
banding, 68
bar pearls, 101
Barguirdjian, Henri, 145
baroque pearls, 39, 44–45,
    65, 72–73, 105
Bear, Ellen, 47
beeswax, tumbling with, 76,
    77

bill of sale (sales receipt),
    171–173, 175
bivalve molluscs, 23
Biwa pearls, 41, 92, 95–96
black pearls
    about, 51–52
    artificial enhancements, 78, 79
    experts' advice, 115–116
    price charts, 108–110
    quality, value and, 70, 71, 93,
    96–98
bleaching/dyeing, of pearls
    drill hole examination, 62,
    70–71
    experts' advice, 122
    freshwater cultured, 42, 43
    misrepresentation and, 81
    techniques, 78–80
Block, John, 148, 153
body color, of pearls, 69, 70,
    71, 95
Boin, Whitney, 164
Book of the Pearl, The, 143
Boucheron, Alain, 134–135
Boucheron, Frederic, 135
Boucheron (jewelry firm),
    134–135
Branellec, Jacques, 116
buffing, of pearls, 77
Bulgari, Nicola, 136–137
Bulgari (jewelry firm), 135–137
Burmese pearls, 51, 91
Burton, Richard, 146
button pearls, 45

C
calcareous concretions, defined,
    25
calcite, 24
calcium carbonate, 24, 54
carat weight, 73–74
caring for pearls, 166–168
Cartier, Louis, 138
Cartier (jewelry firm), 16,
    137–138
Central Gem Laboratory
    (Japan), 182
"chalky" luster, 64, 68, 72
"chance" pearls, 47, 48
chemical bleaching (see bleach-
    ing/dyeing)

China, pearls and, 5, 91–93
chlorine bleach, pearls and,
    166, 167
Chow, Sammy, 144
Christie's International Jewel
    Sales, 148–153
circlé pearls, 49, 72
clasps, for pearls, 160–161
Cleopatra, 14–15
"coin" pearls, 72, 101
color, of pearls (see also black
    pearls; bleaching/dyeing)
    abalone, 53
    American freshwater cultured,
    42, 43–44
    enhancements, artificial, 78–80
    experts' advice, 114, 122–123
    fancy category, 39, 51, 70
    golden/yellow, 94
    natural or cultured, compared,
    31
    quality, value and, 63, 69–71,
    88, 89
    questions to ask, 172–173
conch pearls, 52, 54–55
conchiolin, 23–24, 26, 79
Cook Islands, pearls and, 93
cosmetics/perfumes, pearls and,
    71, 166, 167
cracks/peeling, of pearls, 68, 72,
    115
"crayfish pearls," 25
Crowningshield, Robert, 123
cultivated pearls (see cultured
    pearls)
Cultured Pearl Information
    Center, 187
cultured pearls (see also quality,
    issues of)
    abalone, 52–53
    care/storage of, 166–168
    choosing fine, 87–89,
    118–119, 131–132
    clasps, 160–161
    compared, imitation pearls,
    36–37
    compared, natural pearls,
    26–28, 29–36
    cultivation period, 27, 28–29,
    43, 60

designs, winning, 163–164
experts' advice, 113–133
FTC guidelines, 36, 145
identifying, 34–36
imperfections, causes of, 27,
29, 60, 74
invention/development of,
12–13
men and, 162–163
physical characteristics of, 31,
32–33, 42
price charts, 100–110
processing/treatments, 77–80,
118
production risks/expense of,
27–28, 40
production techniques, 12,
26–30, 41–42, 43–44, 92
shorteners/twisters for, 161
stringing, 159–160, 168
terminology, 171
types/classification categories,
38–39, 62–63, 72
viewing techniques, 63, 65,
68, 71–72, 95
wearing, 159–165
Curiel, François, 148–149

D
Daniel, Jeanne B., 143
D'Elia, Bartholomew, 117–118
Destino, Ralph, 137–138
diamond rondelles, pearls and,
135
domé® pearls, 44, 47, 98
drill holes, examination of, 35,
62, 68, 70, 75, 121–122
Dunay, Henry, 164
dyeing, of pearls (see bleach-
ing/dyeing, of pearls)

E
Elizabeth I, Queen of England,
2, 8, 11–12, 17–18
enhancements, artificial, 76–78
(see also bleaching/dyeing)

F
fancy color category, 39, 51, 70,
172–173

"faux" pearls (see imitation
pearls)
Federal Trade Commission
(FTC) guidelines, 36, 58, 145
flat drop pearls, 101
fraud/misrepresentation, 78, 80,
81–83
French Polynesia, pearls and,
13, 93, 130–131
freshwater molluscs, 23, 25
freshwater pearls (see also
American freshwater pearls)
about, 26, 28, 38, 41–44
price charts, 106
quality, value and, 91–93
types, 45, 46–52
FTC (see Federal Trade
Commission (FTC) guide-
lines)

G
Gem Testing Laboratory of
Great Britain, 182
Gemological Institute of
America (G.I.A.), 177, 181
G.I.A. Gem Trade Laboratory
(GTL), 122, 181, 186
Gould, Florence, 148, 152
Great Britain, Gem Testing
Laboratory, 182
Gubelin Gemological
Laboratory, 182

H
half-pearls (hemisphere pearls),
47, 49, 82
Hanni, Dr. H.A., 118–119
"Hanoverian Pearls," 18
Harry Winston, Inc., 147
Hemmerle, Stefan, 139–140
Hemmerle Juweliere (jewelry
firm), 139–140
"hinges," mollusc, 82
Hope, Henry, 16–17
"Hope Pearl," 16–17
Howell, David, 18–19

I
imitation pearls, 36–37, 58, 83,
89, 171

India, pearls and, 5, 7, 19–20
Indonesia, pearls and, 94–95
insurance appraisals, 176–178
International Gemmological
Institute, 181, 185
irradiation, of pearls, 80, 81,
122
Ishii, Kikuichiro, 142

J
Janot, Bernard, 141
Japan, pearls and, 95–96,
123–124, 182 (see also Akoya
pearls; Biwa pearls)
Japan Pearl Promotion Society,
187
jewelers
experts' advice, 113–133
selection of, 173–175
Jewelry Information Center, 187

K
Kailis, George, 119–120
Kawasake, Kaori, 164
Keshi pearls, 47–48, 91
Kondo, M., 40
Krashes, Laurence S., 147
Krikorian, Krikor, 140
Kunz, George, 143

L
La Pelegrina, 16, 150
La Peregrina, 15–16, 146–147,
154
La Régente, 18, 149–150
laboratory verification
black pearls, 80
getting a report, 179–186
importance of, 122
nacre thickness, 69, 78,
118–119
natural pearls, 36, 82
selecting a lab, 177–178
lacquer-coated pearls, 77–78,
81, 82
Lake Biwa (Japan) (see Biwa
pearls)
Landrigan, Edward, 146–147
Latendresse, John and Gina,
120–122

LeGrand, Paul, 135
Liddicoat, Richard, 122–123
lighting, viewing pearls in,
    35–36, 63, 65, 71, 95
loupe, using a, 61–62, 68
luster
    caring for pearls and, 166–168
    cultured vs. imitation, com-
        pared, 37
    cultured vs. natural, com-
        pared, 31
    defined, 24
    enhancements, artificial, 77–78
    quality, value and, 63, 64–65,
        68, 72, 87–88
    questions to ask, 172

M
mabé pearls, 46–47, 53, 78, 80,
    107
Macnow, Devin, 123–124
"Majorica" pearls, 37
"make," of pearls, 75
Mancini Pearls, The, 2, 151
mantle tissue, 26, 40
matching, of pearls
    natural or cultured, compared,
        31, 33
    quality, value and, 75, 173
Mauboussin, Patrick, 140–141
Mauboussin (jewelry firm),
    140–141
Michiko, Empress of Japan, 141
Mikimoto, Kokichi, 10, 12, 13,
    40, 117–118
Mikimoto (jewelry firm), 142
Mise, Tatsuhei, 12
misrepresentation (see
    fraud/misrepresentation)
Mogul emperors, pearls and,
    19–20
mollusc "hinges," 82
molluscs, 23–26, 52, 54
"mother-of-pearl," 23, 43, 47
"mystery clasp," 160–161

N
nacre
    cultured pearls, 26–30, 41, 92
    mabé pearls, 46–47

natural pearls, 24, 25
    quality, value and, 63, 66–69,
        172, 179–180, 181
natural pearls (see also pearls)
    declining world supply of,
        12–13, 25–26, 30
    freshwater, 42
    identifying, 31, 34–36,
        128–130
    misrepresentation, 82
    organic formation of, 23–26,
        29–30
    physical characteristics of,
        24–25, 31, 32–33
navette pearls, 101
necklace lengths
    price charts, 102–106
    terminology, 165
New World, pearls and, 11–12
Nishikawa, Tokichi, 12
non-nacreous pearls, 54
non-nucleated pearls, 26
nucleus, 26, 29, 40, 74, 79

O
off-center drilling, 75, 121–122
orient
    defined, 24
    experts' advice, 121
    natural or cultured, compared,
        31
    quality, value and, 63, 65–66,
        68, 88
    questions to ask, 172
out-of-round pearls, 44, 60, 72,
    88
overtone, of pearls, 69, 70, 71,
    95
oysters (see molluscs)

P
Paspaley, Nicholas, 124–127
Peacock Throne, 19
pearl reports (see laboratory
    verification)
Pearl Society, The, 187
"Pearl World" (journal), 187
pearlessence, 37, 77–78, 82
pearls (see also cultured pearls;
    natural pearls)
    choosing fine, 87–89, 118–119

discovery of, in New World,
    11–12
experts' advice, 113–133
freshwater, 41–44
history of, 3–13
identifying, 34–36, 128–130
imitation, 36–37
imperfections, causes of, 25,
    30
legendary, tales of, 14–20
as medicinal preparations,
    10–11
misrepresentation, 81–83
questions to ask, 171–175
religious writings and, 8–9
terminology, 36, 145, 171
wedding traditions and, 7–8
word derivation, 6–7
peeling (see cracks/peeling)
perfume (see cosmetics/
    perfumes)
Persian Gulf, 5–6, 12
Philippines, 94–95
Plant, Maisie, 137
polishing, of pearls, 76, 77, 168
pollution, 12, 25, 30
Polynesian pearls (see French
    Polynesia)
"poppy" pearls, 47
"potato" pearls, 65, 72, 92
price charts, 100–110

Q
quality, issues of
    color, 69–71
    examining pearls for, 60–63
    experts' advice, 118
    factors of, 63–64
    importance of, 171–172
    luster, 64–65
    "make"/off-center drilling, 75
    nacre thickness, 66–69
    orient, 65–66
    selecting cultured pearls and,
        59–60, 118–119, 131–132
    shape, 72–73
    size, 73–74
    surface perfection, 71–72
"Queen" Pearl, 18–19

R
reports (*see* laboratory verification)
Richey, William, 164
ringed (circlé) pearls, 49, 72, 98
rosé overtone, 70, 79
round pearls (*see also* out-of-round pearls)
about, 39, 40, 42
misrepresentation, 81–82, 94
quality, value and, 65, 72–73
saltwater/freshwater, 26, 27
royalty, pearls and, 2, 8, 11–12, 14–20

S
saltwater molluscs, 23, 25
saltwater pearls
about, 26, 27, 39–40, 45
price charts, 102–105
quality, value and, 92
types, 46–52
Sara Pearl, The, 150
Saville-Kent, William, 12
Scarratt, Kenneth, 127–128
seed pearls, 47–48
semi-baroque pearls, 72
semi-cultured pearls (*see* imitation pearls)
semi-round pearls, 72
shape, of pearls (*see also* round pearls)
abalone, 53
cultured, freshwater, 42
cultured vs. natural, compared, 31, 33
experts' advice, 113–114
matching and, 44, 75, 173
quality, value and, 64, 72–73
questions to ask, 171
shellfish, 23, 25
Shire, Maurice, 128–130
silver nitrate, 80, 81
simulated pearls (*see* imitation pearls)
size, of pearls
quality, value and, 64, 73–74, 88
questions to ask, 173
solid "blister" pearls, 46, 47, 98

Sotheby's Jewelry Division, 148, 153–156
South Sea Pearl Consortium Ltd., 187
South Sea pearls
about, 40, 50–51
artificial enhancements, 78
experts' advice, 120, 126–127
price charts, 106
quality, value and, 65, 74, 82, 90–91, 94–95
spherical pearls (*see* round pearls)
SSEF Swiss Gemological Laboratory, 182, 184
storing pearls, 166–168
stringing pearls, 159–160, 168
surface perfection (*see also* luster)
enhancements, artificial, 77–78
misrepresentation, 82
quality, value and, 64, 71–72
questions to ask, 173
Switzerland, 182, 184
symmetrical pearls, 39, 45–46, 72–73

T
Tahitian Pearl Association, 187
Tahitian pearls, 96–98, 108–110, 130–131
Takahashi, Koichi, 142
Tavernier, J.B., 19–20
Taylor, Elizabeth, 16, 146
Tennessee, 43, 47, 98
Thailand, 182
three-quarter pearls, 49–50, 81, 94
Tiffany, Charles, 19
Tiffany & Co., 143
Tiffany's "Queen" Pearl, 18–19
tint, of pearls, 69, 70
tissue-graft pearls, 26
tone, of pearl color, 70, 71, 95
"tooth test," 37, 89
torsade, defined, 160, 165
Trio Pearl Company, 144
tumbling, of pearls, 76, 77

U
ultrasonic cleaners, 77, 168
U.S. (*see* American freshwater pearls; Federal Trade Commission (FTC))
univalve molluscs, 52, 54

V
Van Cleef & Arpels, 144–145
Vanderbilt, Grace, 137
Verdura (jewelry firm), 146–147
vinegar, pearls and, 166, 167

W
Wan, Robert, 130–131
water conditions, nacre quality and, 65, 66–67
waxing, of pearls, 76, 77
wedding traditions, pearls and, 7–8
weight, of pearls, 73–74
white color category, 38–39, 70
whitening pearls (*see* bleaching/dyeing)
Winston, Harry, 54, 96, 147
World Pearl Organization, 187

X
x-ray examination, of pearls, 36

Y
Yamamoto, Torio, 131–132

Z
Zucker, Benjamin, 132–133

Buy Your "TOOLS OF THE TRADE . . ." Gem Identification Instruments
directly from GEMSTONE PRESS

Whatever instrument you need, GemStone Press can help. Use the convenient order form below, or contact us directly for assistance.

ITEM / QUANTITY	PRICE EA.*	TOTAL $
Loupes—Professional Jeweler's 10X Triplet Loupes		
_____ Bausch & Lomb 10X Triplet Loupe.	$44.00	$ _____
_____ Standard 10X Triplet Loupe.	$29.00	_____
_____ "The Fill Finder" ™ RosGem Dark-field Loupe..	$174.95	_____
—NEW! Spot filled diamonds, other enhancements and zoning instantly. Operates with large maglite (additional - see below)		
Color Filters		
_____ Chelsea Filter.	$44.95	_____
_____ H-H Synthetic Emerald Filter Set	$32.00	_____
_____ Hanneman Filter Set.	$50.00	_____
Calcite Dichroscope		
_____ RosGem Dichroscope.	$99.00	_____
Diamond Tester		
_____ Diamond Star I Diamond Tester.	$95.00	_____

Complete Pocket Instrument Set
SPECIAL 12% SAVINGS!
BUY THIS ESSENTIAL TRIO AND SAVE $18.00
Used together, you can identify 85% of all gems with these three portable, pocket-sized instruments—the essential trio.
• Standard 10X Triplet Loupe • Chelsea Filter • RosGem Dichroscope
Pocket Instrument Set: With Standard Loupe .... **only $154.95**
With Bausch & Lomb Loupe .... **only $169.95**

Refractometer		
_____ RosGem Model RFA Triplex I 322 Portable Refractometer	$449.00	_____
—operates with small maglight (additional - see below)		
Polariscope		
_____ RosGem Portable Polariscope.	$60.00	_____
—operates with large maglite (additional) or immersion cell light unit (see below)		
Immersion Cell		
_____ RosGem Portable Immersion Cell w/diffused light	$120.00	_____
—operates with small maglite (additional - see below)		
Maglites		
_____ Large Maglite.	$15.00	_____
_____ Small Maglite.	$11.00	_____

Shipping/Insurance per order: $4.95 1st item, $2.00 each add'l item $ _____

* Prices subject to change without notice

TOTAL $ _____

Check enclosed for $_____ (make checks payable to: GEMSTONE Press)

Charge my credit card: ❏ Visa ❏ MasterCard

Name on card _____

Credit Card # _____ Expiration Date _____

Signature _____ Phone (____) _____

Please send book(s) to: Name _____

Street _____

City/State/Zip _____

Phone, mail, or fax orders to: **GEMSTONE Press**, P.O. Box 237, Woodstock, VT 05091
Tel (802) 457-4000 • Fax (802) 457-4004 • Credit card orders (800) 962-4544
Generous Discounts on Quantity Orders

003

Cut along dotted line

Something great just got better!

The "unofficial bible"

NEW! 3rd Edition
JEWELRY & GEMS: THE BUYING GUIDE

by Antoinette L. Matlins, PG *and* A.C. Bonanno, FGA, ASA, MGA

—over 150,000 copies in print—

Updated • Expanded • Revised

JEWELRY & GEMS: THE BUYING GUIDE, 3RD EDITION now has *even more* useful information. Learn the tricks of the trade from *insiders*: how to buy diamonds, pearls, precious and other popular colored gems with confidence and knowledge. More than just a buying guide...discover what's available and what choices you have, what determines quality as well as cost, how to care for and protect valuable gems, what questions to ask before you buy, and what to get in writing. Easy to read and understand. Excellent for staff training.

- Over 1/3 brand new material, including 64 more information-packed pages
- Twice as many beautiful color pages—over 100 color photos—showing dazzling gems, the newest cuts, and beautiful classic and contemporary jewelry by award-winning designers
- Great new sections:
  - DESIGN & STYLE covers classic and innovative settings, tips on getting a larger look, and how to get what you want within your budget
  - GOLD & PLATINUM covers everything you need to know about gold and platinum: colors, finishes, factors affecting cost, underkarating
  - PEARLS covers cultured versus imitation pearls, varieties available, factors affecting value, how to evaluate quality
- Full coverage of exciting new gems recently discovered—"red emerald," neon tourmaline, sunstone, and more
- How to properly read diamond grading reports and colored gem reports
- New treatments—and deceptions—and how to guard against them.

6" x 9", 304 pp., 16 full color pages & over 200 color and b/w illustrations/photos
Hardcover ISBN 0-943763-12-6 **$23.95**   Paperback ISBN 0-943763-11-8 **$16.95**

FOR CREDIT CARD ORDERS CALL 1-800-962-4544

Available from your bookstore or directly from the publisher. TRY YOUR BOOKSTORE FIRST.

Please send me *Jewelry & Gems: The Buying Guide:* ____ copies at $16.95* (pb);
____ copies at $23.95 (hc), plus $3.50 s/h for 1st book, $2.00 ea. add'l book
Check enclosed for $_____ (make checks payable to: GEMSTONE Press)
Charge my credit card: ❑ Visa ❑ Mastercard
Name on card_____
Credit Card #_____Expiration Date_____
Signature_____Phone (____)_____
Please send book(s) to: Name_____
Street_____
City/State/Zip_____

TOTAL SATISFACTION GUARANTEE

If for any reason you're not completely delighted with this book, return it within 30 days for a full refund.

Phone, mail, or fax orders to: GEMSTONE Press, P.O. Box 237, Woodstock, VT 05091
Tel (802) 457-4000 • *Fax* (802) 457-4004 • *Credit card orders* (800) 962-4544
Generous Discounts on Quantity Orders

*Prices subject to change

003

Do You Really Know What You're Buying?
Is It Fake or Is It Real?
If You Aren't Sure, Order Now—

The companion book to Jewelry & Gems: The Buying Guide

GEM IDENTIFICATION MADE EASY

A Hands-On Guide to More Confident Buying and Selling

by **Antoinette L. Matlins**, PG
and **Antonio C. Bonanno**, FGA, ASA, MGA
Authors of *Jewelry & Gems: The Buying Guide* and
Engagement & Wedding Rings:
The Definitive Buying Guide for People in Love

Award Winner

304 pages, 6" x 9", *with more than 150 photographs*
and illustrations, 75 in full color ISBN 0-943763-03-7 **$29.95**

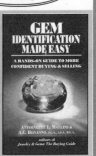

**The first and only book that explains in non-technical terms how to use
pocket, portable and laboratory instruments to identify diamonds and colored gems
and to separate them from imitations and "look-alikes."**

The book's approach is direct and practical, and its style is **easy to understand**. In fact, with this easy-to-use guide, *anyone* can begin to master gem identification.

Using a simple, step-by-step system, the authors explain the proper use of nine essential but uncomplicated instruments that will do the identification tasks, what to look for gemstone by gemstone, and how to set up a basic lab at modest cost. **Three of the instruments are inexpensive, portable, pocket instruments which, when used together, can identify almost 85% of all precious and popular stones.**

Including Complete and Easy Instructions:

➤ **Setting Up a Basic Lab**
➤ **Description of Each Instrument — What It Will Show & How to Use It**
  • Loupe • Chelsea Filter • Electronic Diamond Tester • Refractometer
  • Ultraviolet Lamp • Microscope • Spectroscope • Polariscope • Dichroscope
➤ **Antique and Estate Jewelry** — *The True Test for the Gem Detective*
  • Dyeing • Composite Stones • Foil Backing • Substitutions
➤ **Appendices:** Charts and Tables of Gemstone Properties, Schools, Laboratories,
  Associations, Publications, and Recommended Reading

As entertaining as it is informative. Essential for gem lovers, jewelers, antique dealers, collectors, investors, and hobbyists. "THE BOOK YOU CAN'T DO WITHOUT" —*Rapaport Diamond Report*

FOR CREDIT CARD ORDERS CALL 1-800-962-4544

Available from your bookstore or directly from the publisher. TRY YOUR BOOKSTORE FIRST.

- -

Please send me _____ copies of *Gem Identification Made Easy: A Hands-On
  Guide to More Confident Buying & Selling* at $29.95* plus $3.50 s/h each
Check enclosed for $_____ (make checks payable to: GEMSTONE Press)
Charge my credit card: ❏ Visa ❏ MasterCard
Name on card_____
Credit Card #_____Expiration Date_____
Signature_____Phone (_____)_____
Please send book(s) to: Name_____
Street_____
City/State/Zip_____

**TOTAL
SATISFACTION
GUARANTEE**
If for any reason
you're not
completely
delighted with this
book, return it
within 30 days
for a full
refund.

Phone, mail, or fax orders to: GEMSTONE Press, P.O. Box 237, Woodstock, VT 05091
Tel (802) 457-4000 • *Fax* (802) 457-4004 • *Credit Card Orders* (800) 962-4544   *Price subject to change
Generous Discounts on Quantity Orders

003

At Last! A Book that Removes the Fear and Restores the *Romance*

· COMPREHENSIVE · EASY TO READ · PRACTICAL
The Book Couples In Love Have Been Waiting for...

Engagement & Wedding Rings by *Matlins and Bonanno* tells everything you need to know to design, select, buy and enjoy...to truly experience the wonder and excitement that should be part of it, part of creating that "perfect" ring.

Filled with valuable information. *Engagement & Wedding Rings* will help you make the *right* choice. You will discover:

- Romantic traditions behind engagement and wedding rings
- How to select the right style and design for *you*
- Secrets to the differences in diamonds and colored gemstones that may *appear* to be the same quality
- Steps to compare prices properly
- Tricks to get what you want on a budget
- Ways to add new life to an "heirloom"
- How to select your jeweler, appraiser and insurer
- What to do to protect yourself against fraud and misrepresentation—what to ask and what to get in writing

Dazzling color section of over 130 different rings showing antique to contemporary designs.

Over 400 illustrations and photographs. 304 pages, 6" x 9" Quality softcover.

ISBN 0-943763-05-3. **$14.95**

Makes an ideal gift or premium

This book tells it all...

*Available from your bookstore
—or directly from the publisher
Try your bookstore first.*

softcover only $14.95

FOR TOLL FREE CREDIT CARD ORDERS CALL 1-800-962-4544

Please send me _____ copies of *Engagement & Wedding Rings: The Definitive Buying Guide For People in Love* at $14.95* plus $3.50 s/h each

Check enclosed for $_____ (make checks payable to "GEMSTONE Press")

Charge my credit card: ❑ Visa ❑ Mastercard

Name on card_____

Credit Card #_____Expiration Date_____

Signature_____Phone(_____)_____

Please send book(s) to: Name_____

Street_____

City/State/Zip_____

Phone or mail orders to: GEMSTONE Press, P.O. Box 237, Woodstock, VT 05091

Tel (802) 457-4000 • Fax(802) 457-4004

Generous Discounts on Quantity Orders

TOTAL SATISFACTION GUARANTEE
If for any reason you're not completely delighted with this book, return it within 30 days for a full refund.

*Price subject to change

003

FINALLY! EVERYTHING YOU NEED
TO BUY BEAUTIFUL PEARLS WITH CONFIDENCE

COMPREHENSIVE • EASY TO READ • PRACTICAL
THE PEARL BOOK: THE DEFINITIVE BUYING GUIDE
How to Select, Buy, Care for & Enjoy Pearls

The Pearl Book by *Antoinette L. Matlins, P.G.* is a timely addition to her other internationally acclaimed best-sellers on buying gems and jewelry.

With today's finest cultured pearls rivalling diamond, ruby, emerald and sapphire in terms of popularity, rarity and price, more and more people are searching for a reliable source of information to guide them.

This comprehensive, authoritative guide tells readers everything they need to know about pearls to fully understand and appreciate them, and avoid any unexpected–and costly–disappointments, now and in future generations.

- A journey into the rich history and romance surrounding pearls.
- Differences between natural, cultured, and imitation pearls, and ways to separate them.
- The 5 factors that determine pearl value.
- How to judge pearl quality, including tips on how to see differences with the naked eye.
- How to wear and care for pearls.
- Magnificent pearl creations from the world's leading jewelers.
- Comparisons of all types of pearls, in every size and color, from every pearl-producing country in the world.
- What to look for, what to look out for: How to spot fakes
- Treatments: Good and bad
- Important resource information, including pearl glossary, size charts, sample lab reports, and more...

Special Feature: Exclusive interviews with the world's leading authorities on pearls, who offer "insider" insights and advice.

6" x 9", 232 pages, 16 full color pages & over 250 color and b/w illus./photos
Quality Paperback ISBN 0-943763-15-0 **$19.95** *

Makes an ideal gift or premium

Available from your bookstore —or directly from the publisher. TRY YOUR BOOKSTORE FIRST.

NEW

FOR CREDIT CARD ORDERS CALL 1-800-962-4544

Please send me _____ copies of *The Pearl Book: The Definitive Buying Guide*
at *$19.95* * plus $3.50 for 1st book, $2.00 each additional book

Check enclosed for $_____ (make checks payable to: GEMSTONE Press)
Charge my credit card: ❑ Visa ❑ MasterCard
Name on card_____
Credit Card #_____Expiration Date_____
Signature_____Phone (_____)_____
Please send book(s) to: Name_____
Street_____
City/State/Zip_____

Phone or mail orders to: GEMSTONE Press, P.O. Box 237, Woodstock, VT 05091
Tel (802) 457-4000 • Fax (802) 457-4004 • Credit card orders (800) 962-4544
Generous Discounts on Quantity Orders

TOTAL SATISFACTION GUARANTEE

If for any reason you're not completely delighted with this book, return it within 30 days for a full refund.

*Price subject to change

003

GEMSTONE PRESS
Helping Consumers and the Gem Trade Increase Their Understanding, Appreciation And Enjoyment of Jewelry, Gems and Gemology

An international source for books, gem identification instruments and other items designed to help people in the gem trade and consumers learn more about jewelry, gems and gemology.

GemStone Press books are easy to read, easy to use. Designed for the person who does not have a scientific or technical background, titles include:

✦ **Jewelry & Gems: The Buying Guide** — How to Buy Diamonds, Pearls, Colored Gemstones, Gold & Jewelry with Confidence and Knowledge.

Easy to read ✦ Easy-to-Understand ✦ Practical ✦ Complete Instant Answers... to All Your Questions

More than just a buying guide... Know what you want, know what you're buying, save money and avoid costly mistakes.

"Restores the magic! This book is going to entertain and enlighten all its readers and save some from heartbreak."
—Paul Harvey, Paul Harvey News
"The 'unofficial bible' for the gem investor."
—The Robb Report

✦ **Engagement & Wedding Rings: The Definitive Buying Guide For People in Love** — Tells everything you need to know to design, select, buy and enjoy . . . to truly experience the wonder and excitement that should be part of it, part of creating that "perfect ring."

Available from your bookstore or directly from the Publisher

✦ **Gem Identification Made Easy: A Hands-On Guide to More Confident Buying & Selling** — Learn how to use the "tools of the trade." This book makes gem identification fun and interesting rather than "tedious" — even for those without scientific inclination!

"Useful . . . for the professional and not intimidating for the amateur."
—Diamond Insight

✦ **The Pearl Book: The Definitive Buying Guide** — How to Select, Buy, Care for & Enjoy Pearls
Everything you need to buy beautiful pearls with confidence.

GemStone Press also assists its readers by offering **jeweler's loupes, color filters and other instruments** to help identify and enjoy gems. See information pages in this book or call us for more information.

GEMSTONE PRESS
P.O. BOX 237, WOODSTOCK, VT 05091
TEL: (802) 457-4000 ✦ FAX: (802) 457-4004 ✦ CREDIT CARD ORDERS: (800) 962-4544

Try your bookstore first

Please send me, at no charge, a *FREE* copy of *After You Buy: Tips on Gem & Jewelry Care & Protection* and a *FREE* GEMSTONE Press Catalog.

I am particularly interested in the following subjects (check all that apply):
❑ Diamonds ❑ Colored Stones ❑ Pearls ❑ Jewelry Design
❑ Antique Jewelry ❑ Seminars/Workshops
❑ Costume Jewelry ❑ Periodic Price Guides
❑ Gemstone Cutting ❑ Videotapes ❑ Jewelry Appraising
❑ Other_____

My name_____

Street _____

City/State_____ ZIP _____

For additional copies of
After You Buy: Tips on Gem & Jewelry Care & Protection
Send $5.00 and a *large* stamped, self addressed envelope for each copy to:

GEMSTONE Press
P.O. Box 237, Woodstock, VT 05091

PRL 4/96

Please send me **JEWELRY & GEMS: THE BUYING GUIDE —**
_____ copies at $16.95* (Quality paperback)   _____copies at $23.95* (Hardcover)
plus $3.50 postage and handling for the 1st book, $2.00 each additional book.

Please send me _____ copies of **ENGAGEMENT & WEDDING RINGS: THE DEFINITIVE BUYING GUIDE FOR PEOPLE IN LOVE** at $14.95***
plus $3.50 postage and handling for the 1st book, $2.00 each additional book.

Please send me_____ copies of **GEM IDENTIFICATION MADE EASY: A HANDS-ON GUIDE TO MORE CONFIDENT BUYING & SELLING** at $29.95***
plus $3.50 postage and handling for the first book, $2.00 each additional book.

Please send me_____ copies of **THE PEARL BOOK: THE DEFINITIVE BUYING GUIDE** at $19.95***
plus $3.50 postage and handling for the 1st book, $2.00 each additional book.

Check enclosed for $_____ (*make checks payable to:* GEMSTONE Press)
Charge my credit card: ❑ Visa ❑ MasterCard
Name on card _____
Credit Card #_____ Expiration Date_____
Signature _____ Phone (_____)_____
Please send book(s) to: Name_____
Street_____
City/State/Zip _____

Phone, mail, or fax orders to: GEMSTONE **Press**, P.O. Box 237, Woodstock, VT 05091
Tel (802) 457-4000 • *Fax* (802) 457-4004 • *Credit card orders* (800) 962-4544
Generous Discounts on Quantity Orders

*Price subject to change   *Try Your Bookstore First*   003

Buy Your "TOOLS OF THE TRADE . . ."
Gem Identification Instruments
directly from GEMSTONE PRESS

Whatever instrument you need, GemStone Press can help. Use the convenient order form below, or contact us directly for assistance.

ITEM / QUANTITY	PRICE EA.*	TOTAL $
Loupes—Professional Jeweler's 10X Triplet Loupes		
_____ Bausch & Lomb 10X Triplet Loupe.	$44.00	$ _____
_____ Standard 10X Triplet Loupe.	$29.00	_____
_____ "The Fill Finder" ™ RosGem Dark-field Loupe..	$174.95	_____
—NEW! Spot filled diamonds, other enhancements and zoning instantly. Operates with large maglite (additional - see below)		
Color Filters		
_____ Chelsea Filter.	$44.95	_____
_____ H-H Synthetic Emerald Filter Set	$32.00	_____
_____ Hanneman Filter Set.	$50.00	_____
Calcite Dichroscope		
_____ RosGem Dichroscope.	$99.00	_____
Diamond Tester		
_____ Diamond Star I Diamond Tester...............	$95.00	_____

Complete Pocket Instrument Set
SPECIAL 12% SAVINGS!
BUY THIS ESSENTIAL TRIO AND SAVE $18.00
Used together, you can identify 85% of all gems with these three portable, pocket-sized instruments—the essential trio.
• Standard 10X Triplet Loupe • Chelsea Filter • RosGem Dichroscope
Pocket Instrument Set: With Standard Loupe .... **only $154.95**
With Bausch & Lomb Loupe .... **only $169.95**

Refractometer		
_____ RosGem Model RFA Triplex I 322 Portable Refractometer	$449.00	_____
—operates with small maglight (additional - see below)		
Polariscope		
_____ RosGem Portable Polariscope.	$60.00	_____
—operates with large maglite (additional) or immersion cell light unit (see below)		
Immersion Cell		
_____ RosGem Portable Immersion Cell w/diffused light	$120.00	_____
—operates with small maglite (additional - see below)		
Maglites		
_____ Large Maglite.	$15.00	_____
_____ Small Maglite.	$11.00	_____
Shipping/Insurance per order: $4.95 1st item, $2.00 each add'l item		$ _____

* Prices subject to change without notice

TOTAL $ _____

Check enclosed for $_____ (make checks payable to: GEMSTONE Press)
Charge my credit card: ❏ Visa ❏ MasterCard
Name on card_____
Credit Card #_____Expiration Date_____
Signature_____Phone (_____)_____
Please send book(s) to: Name_____
Street_____
City/State/Zip_____

Phone, mail, or fax orders to: GEMSTONE Press, P.O. Box 237, Woodstock, VT 05091
Tel (802) 457-4000 • Fax (802) 457-4004 • Credit card orders (800) 962-4544
Generous Discounts on Quantity Orders

003

Cut along dotted line